SMUGGLER

BY THE SAME AUTHOR
A Dorset Soldier: the Autobiography of Sergeant William Lawrence

SMUGGLER

John Rattenbury
and his Adventures in
Devon, Dorset and Cornwall
1778-1844

(including *Memoirs of a Smuggler, 1837*)

Eileen Hathaway

SHINGLEPICKER PUBLICATIONS
Swanage

© Eileen Hathaway 1994
ISBN 0 9522782 0 0

First published in the UK by
SHINGLEPICKER PUBLICATIONS
28 Bonfields Avenue
Swanage
Dorset BH19 1PL

British Library Cataloguing-in-Publication Data
A catalogue record for this book is available from the British Library

Printed in Great Britain by:
Henry Ling Ltd
The Dorset Press
Dorchester
Dorset

TABLE OF CONTENTS

ILLUSTRATIONS

MAPS

ACKNOWLEDGEMENTS

Many people have been of help to me in producing this book, but special thanks must go to Mrs M Howe of the Devon Record Office, and Ian Maxted of the Westcountry Studies Library, Exeter; also the staff at Swanage Library, the Public Record Office in Kew, the County Record Office in Dorchester, and Bridport Museum.

Reproduced here with the kind permission of the Controller of Her Majesty's Stationery Office are extracts of Crown copyright material from the 18th and 19th Century copy letterbooks of the Custom Houses of Cowes, Dartmouth, Exeter, Lyme and Weymouth, which are held at the Public Record Office, Kew.

Quotations from Reverend John Swete's diary, excerpts from the *Exeter Flying Post* and *Devon Notes Queries Vol.IV*, are included with the permission of the Devon Record Office, and I have to thank the County Record Office in Dorchester for allowing me to quote from the letter about impressment sent in 1787 to the Mayor of Lyme.

Devon County Council and the Westcountry Studies Library have generously allowed me to include the prints on pages 14, 17, 20, 76, 78, 102, 107, 141, 152 and 158, and I am extremely grateful to HM Customs and Excise in Salford for allowing me to reproduce the photographs which appear on pages 12, 34, 51, 66, 95, 110 and 115.

And thank you Roger Guttridge for allowing me to make use of the lists of West Country smugglers you compiled for your book *Dorset Smugglers*.

The painting of John Rattenbury was specially created for the cover of this book by Purbeck artist Dawn Waring.

INTRODUCTION

Throughout his life, John Rattenbury earned his living on the sea, sometimes as a fisherman, sometimes as a pilot, occasionally as a merchant seaman, but mostly as a smuggler. As a smuggler he became so notorious that an enterprising Sidmouth printer prevailed upon him to relate some of his adventures for a book. The result was *Memoirs of a Smuggler*, published in 1837. It was a slim volume which gave contemporary readers tantalising glimpses of smuggling activities in the West Country in the first four decades of the 19th Century. But glimpses were all they could be. Writing within a year of his last acknowledged venture, Rattenbury had to protect the identities of former associates, some of whom were still smuggling, and therefore said little about smuggling activities in which he was not directly involved. He is virtually silent about the methods used to transport the contraband inland after it had been landed, and about the places it was hidden. The effect is a narrative which frustrates through omission. My aim in producing this publication is to offer the modern reader more than Rattenbury does, and you will therefore find on these pages not only his sketchy canvas but much of the detail and colour he left out.

Rattenbury lived in Beer so the emphasis is on that village and its environs, but he travelled far during his lifetime. His voyages as a youth - some of them aboard privateers - took him as far south as Portugal and the Azores, as far east as Gothenburg, and as far west as New York and Newfoundland.

As a smuggler Rattenbury conveyed contraband from the Channel Islands and Cherbourg, and was intimate with the coast from Portsmouth and the Isle of Wight to Falmouth. At the peak of his career his operations were variously centred around Weymouth and Portland, Lyme, Seaton and Beer, Sidmouth, and Dartmouth; and he had skirmishes with customs men and press gangs in places as far apart as Cowes, Bridport, Newton Abbot, Dawlish, Teignmouth and Falmouth. His escapades were many, avoiding a prison sentence in Bodmin jail only by escaping on his way there.

Over 150 years have passed since Rattenbury told his story. There is no longer any need to be coy about identifying his smuggling associates, or others in Devon and Dorset who may have taken part in, or made a living from, this illicit trade. And they *can* be identified. Rattenbury's memoirs contain the only *published* versions of the smuggling incidents in which he took part, but they are not the *only* versions which exist. Smuggling involved smugglers *and* customs officials. Smugglers rarely kept records, but customs officials did and some of their reports and testimonies have survived. These I have used to complement and explain Rattenbury's own account.

For inclusion in this book, the 1837 edition of *Memoirs of a Smuggler* has been edited. Where a chronological error has been uncovered and the evidence for an alternative date overwhelming, it has been noted. Where there is doubt about a placename, the likely alternative appears in the text in square brackets. Some placenames have changed since 1837 so the modern name is given, as are minor explanations of obscure words or text.

It is not obvious from his account, but Rattenbury was illiterate and probably dictated his story to his publisher. The adventures he describes are, as my research has confirmed, undoubtedly his, but some passages in the 1837 edition may owe more to the pen of the publisher than to the powers of composition of the smuggler.

Another factor on which his illiteracy has a bearing is the spelling of his name. He is known today (and in his *Memoirs*) as Rattenbury, but in Customs records and other contemporary archive material, he is consistently referred to as John Ra**dd**enbury. Searches in public record offices can prove fruitless unless a researcher acknowledges and makes allowance for the fact that in the past the spelling of names was erratic.

Whether as John Raddenbury, or John Rattenbury, I commend his story to you, not just as a factual and entertaining personal narrative, but as a window on history through which you will see recreated the smuggling village of Beer in the late 18th and early 19th Centuries, knowing that such scenes were repeated in other villages around the south-west coast of England.

John Rattenbury was a remarkable man. He survived privateering ventures, impressment, imprisonment, shipwreck and storm. His story is remarkable because it survived his illiteracy. What is not so remarkable, as this volume will demonstrate, is that at the time he lived, John Rattenbury was a smuggler.

Eileen Hathaway
1994

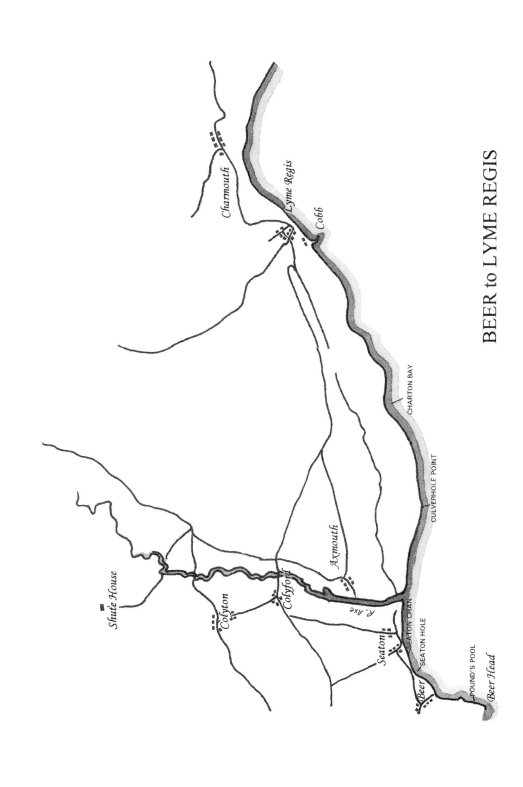

BEER to LYME REGIS

Charmouth

Lyme Regis

Cobb

CHARTON BAY

CULVERHOLE POINT

Shute House

Colyton

Colyford

Axmouth

R. Axe

Seaton

SEATON CHAN

SEATON HOLE

Beer

POUND'S POOL

Beer Head

CHAPTER 1

Beer and the Rattenburys
1745-1793

John Rattenbury was born in Beer, Devon and baptised on 18 October 1778 as John Raddenbury. His father, also called John, was a shoemaker, or 'cordwainer' as they were then called, from Honiton in Devon, where his family had lived since about 1700. It is not known how long John Snr resided in Beer, but it was long enough to court a local girl, Anne Newton, whom he married on 10 November 1777.

Prior to the industrial revolution, populations in rural areas were more static than they are today - the same surnames appear in the Seaton and Beer parish records century after century. The Newtons were there in 1595, and the Abbots, Westlakes, Gibbs, and Loveridges almost as long. By the early 19th Century, smuggling had become a way of life for some families living in the coastal villages of south-west England. Beer in particular acquired a reputation as a notorious haunt of smugglers long before John Rattenbury - its most famous practitioner - was born. In 1747, the situation was so desperate that the local revenue officials - the riding officers - were reinforced by dragoons, eight soldiers being posted in Beer, four in Seaton and another four at Branscombe. But it was on the shoulders of the riding officers themselves that the most arduous responsibilities of prevention rested.

There were few jobs more dangerous than being a riding officer. In 1755, John Hurley of Branscombe died in a 'fall' from the cliff after going to investigate a fire which had been lit to warn off a smuggling vessel at sea. Not long after his death, Nicholas Bools, the riding officer in Beer, was issued with a pair of pistols and a sword by the Custom House. It was not unusual for arms to be issued to preventive men in times of crisis, then recalled when the threat of violence diminished. This must have happened frequently because, in the West country in the 18th Century, smuggling was carried out on a vast scale, and large gangs of men roamed the countryside in open defiance of the customs officials they outnumbered. The 'Beere' gang was one of them. On 30 August 1760, the official in charge of the Custom House at Exeter - the collector - informed the Board in London that:

'The greatest part of the smuggling on this coast is carried on by the Beere Boats who generally run their goods on the Western side and shore of Torbay, within the Port of Dartmouth, at a place

called Livermead, where we have been informed that lately [was] landed great quantities of goods; that not less than fifty or sixty men came there and were employed all the night in carrying away the goods, and that most of these men had some kind of offensive weapons or other." (PRO. Exeter Letterbooks CUST 64/4)

A few months later, in December 1760, 25 members, mounted on horseback, shepherded thirty horses laden with contraband tea into Exeter by the west gate and rode unmolested, through the city to their markets beyond. In April 1766, after another landing, forty of the gang, accompanying fifty horses loaded with tea, encountered a group of customs officers, which included William Hunt. Outnumbered, the customs men withdrew, but Hunt was not quick enough. Caught and injured, he later had to have his dislocated shoulder put back by the force of a cider press.

The peak year for smuggling in Devon was 1782 when twenty-five armed vessels of up to 100 tons each, manned by crews of up to twenty men, were regularly carrying goods into the Exeter area. 1,248,000 gallons of brandy and 806,400lbs of tea, were smuggled in during the previous three years - 90% of the quantity consumed.

1. A Revenue cutter (the Greyhound*) of 1760*

Warren Lisle, an experienced customs official, suspected that the four revenue cutters operating between St. Alban's Head in Dorset and Berry Head in Torbay had agreements with the smugglers, and that by 'contenting themselves with a small part from the smuggler', they allowed 'the greater part to be run ashore'. Given the size of the smuggling vessels, and the fact that the crews were not only armed with weapons but prepared to use them, the reluctance of the revenue cutter commanders to confront them is hardly to be wondered at.

Conditions were no less hazardous for officers operating on land. In November 1787, at Roncombe Gate, two Excise men were murdered. The following statement, issued from Whitehall, appeared in the *Exeter Flying Post* on 29 November:

> *"Whereas it has been humbly represented to the King, that on Friday Evening, the 2nd Day of November Instant, a most inhuman Murder was committed on the bodies of William Jenkins and William Scott, late Officers in his Majesty's Excise, by a Gang of Smugglers, when the said Officers were in the Execution of their Duty, in attempting to seize some Run Goods, at a Place called Roncombe's Girt, on the Road between Honiton and Beer, in the County of Devon."*

William Voisey was named as one of the murderers, and a pardon was promised to the smuggler who gave the names of Voisey's accomplices, with the further inducement of a reward of £200 to be paid on conviction.

This then was the state of smuggling in east Devon towards the end of the 18th Century when John Rattenbury was born, and when Beer was a small close-knit community of a few hundred people in extended and interrelated families, some with smuggling connections.

But what was Beer like to the casual observer? The Reverend John Swete visited it when travelling through south Devon on horseback in the summer of 1794. He noted his observations in a diary. One night he stayed at an inn in Seaton, moving on next morning to Beer,

> *"a small town consisting of one street which terminated in a pebbly strand. The scenery around this place was bold and romantic, the cliffs in particular hovering high, whilst the fishing boat passing from or entering the cove, with its white sail arresting a beam of light whilst scudding beneath the shaded rock, was productive of one of the most pleasing effects that a water view can afford. Some of the houses of Beer, being built of freestone from the neighbouring quarries, had a decent appearance, and many of their fronts were decorated in the most charming manner with myrtles, in high bloom and luxuriance, which perfumed the air with their delicate odours."*

2. Beer harbour in 1829

Beer was not just a fishing village; it also had a stone industry. Swete says:

> *'I came to the Quarry mouth. At this sight I was exceedingly surprised, for not having had any previous intimation of what I was to see, I had pictured to myself immense rocks, which by the labour of ages had received the form of cliffs, of vast height and unusual magnificence. What then was my disappointment when I beheld the mouth of a cave only before me. Miners lighting up their farthing candles proposed to conduct us through the subterranean.'* (Devon Record Office, 564M)

The stone from the quarry went into the building of the local houses, and it was in such a house, sixteen years before Swete's visit, that the subject of this book was born. This is how John Rattenbury begins his own story:

> I was born at Beer in Devon in 1778. My father, a shoemaker, went on board a man-of-war before I was born and my mother never heard of him again. But she was frugal and industrious, and by selling fish supported us without receiving the least assistance from the parish or any of her friends.

Beer, where we resided, lay open to the sea so I was continually by the water-side. As almost all I saw or heard was connected with that element, I acquired a partiality for it and, almost from my infancy, was determined to be a sailor.

When I was about nine years old, I asked my uncle to let me go fishing with him, to which he consented. Another lad about the same age went with us, and we were continually trying to outdo each other in feats of skill and dexterity. I mention this because I think it had a considerable effect in deciding the cast of my character, and influencing the subsequent events of my life.

I was with my uncle for some time. When we separated it was as a result of an accident which happened in Lyme, where we had gone to sell fish. My uncle and his son, and another man, went on shore to dispose of the fish in the market, leaving me to take care of the boat. The boat got aground and I lost the rudder. When my uncle returned and heard what had happened, he flew into a violent passion, and beat me so severely with the end of a rope that I resolved to leave him, which I did as soon as I returned to Beer.

A few days later I met on the beach a Brixham fisherman who offered to take me as an apprentice if I was inclined. I consented to go on trial and remained with him more than twelve months.

Rattenbury's father was probably impressed. In the 18th Century, during times of peace, the navy's strength was only a fraction of what was needed in time of war, therefore an outbreak of hostilities usually found the Fleet paralysed by undermanning. With no organised system of recruitment, each individual captain, in order to make up his numbers, would try to induce men to join by paying them a bounty. As there were never enough volunteers, the press gangs were called out to force men into serving. The duties of these press gangs were eventually taken over by the Admiralty's Impress Service, but the element of compulsion remained.

Theoretically, the gangs could only impress seamen into the navy but, in practice, they took any able-bodied man available. In provincial areas, they expected the co-operation of government officials, as can be seen from this warrant issued to the Mayor of Lyme by the Admiralty in 1787.

'In pursuance of His Majesty's Order in Council dated the 19th Day of September 1787, We do hereby Impower and Direct you to Impress as many Seamen of strong Bodies and in good Health as you possibly can procure, giving to each Man so Impressed One Shilling for Prest-Money. And in the Execution hereof you are to take Care not to demand or receive any Money, Gratuity, Reward, or other Consideration whatsoever, for the Sparing, Exchanging, or Discharging any Person or Persons Impressed, or to be Impressed,

as you will answer it at your Peril. This Warrant to continue in Force till the 31st Day of December 1787. And, in the due Execution of this Warrant... all Mayors, Sheriffs, Justices of the Peace, Bailiffs, Constables, Headboroughs, and all other His Majesty's Officers and Subjects, whom it may concern, are hereby required to be aiding and assisting you." (County Record Office, Dorchester. Photocopy 178)

In 1776, the navy's strength was 28,000 men, but by 1779, after the outbreak of the American War of Independence, the number had swollen to 70,000, and that included John Raddenbury Senior, whose wife was expecting their first child. What happened to Raddenbury is not known. The information may be buried in naval muster books and casualty lists at the Public Record Office, but it is of no use now to poor Anne Raddenbury, who found herself in the unenviable position of having to bring up her baby son without the benefit of a husband's support, the navy having made a widow of her in all but name,

Anne did not remarry, but she may have taken a common law husband because, in 1786 when she was thirty-five and her son eight, she gave birth to a bastard daughter called Elizabeth. It was soon after that John started going fishing with his uncle, so was this uncle really an uncle, or was he Anne Raddenbury's consort?

John Raddenbury Snr was from Honiton. He was the first Raddenbury to be registered in Beer therefore it is unlikely that the uncle was a Raddenbury, so was he a Newton? If Rattenbury's mother was the Anne Newton born to Joseph and Mary Newton in March 1751 then she did not have a brother. However, if she was the Ann Newton born to Richard and Grace Newton in August 1748, then her brother was John Newton, born to the same couple in June 1742. During the 1780s and 1790s, the name John Newton crops up frequently in the shipping registers of Lyme and Exeter as the master of various vessels with Beer and Seaton connections.

A few days after he left his uncle, John says he became an apprentice to a Brixham fisherman. This would have been about 1790 when Brixham, with a population of about 4000, was the foremost fishing port on the south coast, and the home of a new type of trawler believed to have been developed at this time, or soon after. The Brixham Trawler was one of the most powerful sailing vessels of its size ever built. It was the prototype for the fishing boats in the huge fleets which later became established on the north-eastern coast of England in places like Hull and Grimsby. Rattenbury's master was at the forefront of Brixham's flourishing fishing trade:

> He had a great many apprentices, all older than myself, and they used me very roughly, which made my situation very uncomfortable. One day, having been treated worse than usual, I decided to endure it

no longer. A vessel belonging to Beer was then at Brixham so I went to the captain and asked if he would give me a passage back to my native place, which he kindly agreed to.

When I got home, I was very disappointed to find that I could not get any employment, so I proceeded to Bridport where the master of a vessel engaged me to go with him in the coasting trade from Bridport to Dartmouth. I remained with him only a short time because war had broken out between England and France. So afraid was he of the press gang that, one morning at 4 o'clock, he left the vessel. Not liking to continue on board alone, I left with him, and returned to Beer.

3. Brixham from Heath Common 1825

Bridport in Dorset, about fifteen miles to the east of Beer, was a busy port, its leading citizens being merchants of the Colfox, Downe and Hounsell families. They were also ship-owners, frequently in partnership with one another. The ships they owned were increasingly built in Bridport itself by the team of Henry and William Good so, although only a boy, Rattenbury was establishing shipping contacts as far apart at Dartmouth and Bridport, and was familiarising himself with the coast between the two.

CHAPTER 2

Privateer and Prisoner
1793-1795

In February 1793 England again went to war with France. Two months later, the 'hottest press every remembered' took place. So stripped of their crews were some of the merchant ships anchored in the Thames, that they could not sail. Experienced seaman, like the Bridport captain, sought to elude the press gangs by removing themselves from the places of greatest danger - the ports. For those who succeeded, the war brought increased employment opportunities because local merchants, like the Downes of Bridport and the Horsfords of Weymouth, began to buy vessels and fit them out to send privateering.

In the 18th Century, privateering was an accepted part of Britain's war effort. It was a form of government-approved piracy directed against enemy shipping. Ship owners could apply for a licence, called a Letter of Marque, which gave them permission to seize French merchant ships in the name of the King. In 1793, the Admiralty lost no time issuing them:

> *"Whereas, by his Majesty's Commission under the Great Seal of Great Britain bearing the Date of the 14th Day of February 1793,... we are required and authorised to issue forth and grant Letters of Marque and Reprisals to any of His Majesty's Subjects or others, whom we shall deem fitly qualified in that Behalf, for apprehending, seizing, and taking, the Ships, Vessels and Goods belonging to France, or to any Persons being Subjects of France, or inhabiting within any of the Territories of France; and to bring the same to Judgement in any of His Majesty's Courts of Admiralty."*

On the licence was entered the name of the vessel, its tonnage, its firepower, how many crew it could muster, and the name of the commander, who was exhorted to:

> *"keep an exact Journal of his Proceedings, and therein particularly to take Notice of all Prizes which shall be taken by him, the Nature of such Prizes, the Time and Place of their being taken, the Value of them as near as he can judge, as also the Situation, Motion and Strength of the French, as well as he can discover by the best Intelligence he can get; of which he is, from Time to Time*

as he shall have Opportunity, to transmit an Account to our Secretary." (PRO. ADM7/328)

Some of the first people to apply for and be granted Letters of Marque were commanders of vessels in the revenue service. One was Captain Francis Sarman of the *Swan*, based at Cowes. Another was Thomas Amos of the *Swallow*. Guernsey and Alderney merchants were well placed to take advantage of the development, and were soon fitting out cutters like the *Lively*, commanded by Du Bois Smith.

The spur for all this activity was profit. Privateering could be lucrative with a large percentage of the proceeds from the sale of captured French ships and cargos going to the ship's owners, and substantial shares in prize money being distributed to the captain and his crew. But it was also a very risky enterprise. French merchants operated privateers too, so the hunter could become the hunted. Crews of both countries were captured and held prisoner. In the 1790s exchanges were quickly arranged, the men usually being liberated within a year.

Ships of other countries were not immune from commercial piracy. As allies of France, American and Spanish vessels were particularly vulnerable to attack by the British. So brisk was the trade between Europe and the New World that English privateers found the North Atlantic a good hunting ground, and used the neutral Portuguese islands of the Azores to re-supply their vessels.

At the outbreak of war in February 1793, Rattenbury was a boy of fourteen with no experience of either war or privateering. He did, however, have an understandable fear of impressment, which is why he left Bridport for the safety of Beer. There he found an opportunity awaiting him.

> On my arrival at Beer I found that my uncle was busy engaging men for a scheme then much talked of - privateering. As this enterprise pleased my roving fancy, I immediately entered, and with twenty-two others, men and boys, I was conveyed in a small fishing sloop to Torquay, and put on the *Dover*, commanded by Captain Mathews.

The *Dover* was a lugger of 66 tons with a crew of forty men, commanded by John Mathews. It was granted a Letter of Marque on 11 April 1793.

> For a few days we were active getting the lugger ready for sea, but this was soon done for we were eager at the prospect of the prizes we would take, and the glory we would acquire.
>
> About the latter end of March 1793, we set off on our first cruise off the Western islands [the Azores]. Even now, notwithstanding the lapse of years, I can recall the triumph and exultation which rushed through

4. Harbour, and View of Torquay from the west, 1818

my veins as I saw the shores of my native country recede, and the vast ocean opening before me. Like a bird escaping from its cage, I felt free. I considered those who had risen from the lowest to the highest posts, from the cabin boy to the admiral's flag. I too wished to make my mark. My hopes and expectations were as restless and boundless as the element around me.

After six weeks at sea, we put into Terceira [one of the larger islands in the Azores], to take in provisions and water. After four days we set out on another cruise, during which we fell in with three American merchant ships laden with French goods. Their commanders argued that the ships were not lawful prize so they were allowed to proceed, but as they were later taken by English cruisers, I suspect some underhand dealing between the American captains and our officers.

We continued at sea six or seven weeks. For part of the time we were on short allowances. When our provisions were nearly exhausted we bore away again for Terceira to take in a fresh supply.

On our voyage there we spied a ship to our leeward and decided to bear down on her to find out what she was. When we came up with her we saw she carried English colours, so our captain ordered all hands to go aloft and give her three cheers. As we were preparing to do so, the crew hauled down their English colours and hoisted French ones instead. They then fired two shots at us, one going through our jib, the other between our fore and main-mast. As the French ship mounted 26 guns, resistance was out of the question and escape impossible, so we were obliged to submit quietly to our fate.

The French captain sent a boat alongside our vessel to take off our crew, who were immediately ironed two and two. They were sent down into the lower hold, where they found fifty other English prisoners, captured out of a South Sea merchantman. Being a boy, I was ordered to stand by a gun on the quarter deck. There I remained till 5 o'clock in the evening, when I was sent below to join my companions. The next morning two other boys were taken out of irons, and the three of us were appointed to attend to the prisoners, each having a certain number allotted to his charge.

These poor men were in a deplorable situation for their provisions were bad, and the space in which they were confined was very narrow. I was only a boy, but I felt for them. To try to mitigate their sufferings, I watched for every opportunity to carry below to my shipmates all the provisions I could procure. This usually happened when the French sailors were on deck.

The French captain steered for Bordeaux. After about a fortnight, two frigates appeared in view. I was standing on the deck at the time, near the boatswain, and he, supposing the frigates to be English, said to me in my own language, "It is your turn today, boy, but tomorrow it will be mine".

As soon as I could I went below and told my comrades the news. They were overjoyed, but alas their joy was of short duration for a fog came on, and by the next morning we had totally lost sight of the frigates. This cast a gloom over the countenances of my companions.

That day, towards evening, we sailed up the Garonne, and on the following day entered the port of Bordeaux. We were taken on shore and marched, ironed two and two, to the prison there. So ended the enterprise on which we had all embarked with such enthusiasm. Instead of returning to our native country laden with riches and adorned with trophies, we had, in just a few months, become unwilling guests in a strange land, and exchanged the sweets of freedom for the galling fetters of captivity, the pleasant homes of our fathers for a foreign gaol.

Our situation in captivity was less deplorable than we expected for the prison was airy and commodious, and the French people treated us with kindness and humanity. Sometimes, the keeper sent me to his house to fetch wine for my fellow-prisoners, and in just a few weeks I became such a favourite with him and his wife that I received the greater part of my food from their table. I was even permitted to walk abroad in the city, providing I did not exceed the time fixed for my return, which in summer was 7 o'clock.

Despite this partiality, and their kindness, and although I could appreciate the fine buildings, extensive quay, and beautiful environs for which Bordeaux is so celebrated, I could not forget my native land, and felt such a strange yearning for home that I was always contriving plans for my escape.

EUROPE

I had become acquainted with the master of an American vessel called the *George*. One evening, I was so engaged in conversation with him that I was late back, whereupon the keeper of the prison chided me severely and gave me two or three kicks. He would not allow me to walk out again without receiving his permission in writing, so I decided to carry out a plan I had long thought about. My opportunity came when he was in the garden. I went to the sentry and showed him a ticket I had been given on a former occasion, but which he had neglected to take. As I hoped, he did not examine the date and allowed me to pass. I hastened to a coffee-house where I found the American captain and asked him to take me on board his vessel. To my great joy, he agreed.

The vessel lay in Bordeaux harbour and there I lay concealed for about a month, unable to learn whether any particular inquiry had been made after me. After that, I went ashore with the crew. As I was not apprehended my fears gradually subsided. On occasion though I offended Captain Prowse, and then he would threaten to deliver me up, which used to terrify me not a little.

We remained at Bordeaux a year because of an embargo on all foreign shipping, but as soon as it was removed we took on a cargo of wine etc., and sailed for New York. We arrived after a middling passage of 45 days. The cargo was discharged and the ship's company paid off. Captain Prowse had taken a liking to me and offered to take me on as an apprentice. I was not inclined to accept his proposal, but stayed at New York a few days, examining what was remarkable in the place, and engaging in such amusements as it afforded.

One evening I arranged to meet my late shipmates in a house of public resort in the city and there, as a token of their respect, they each presented me with a dollar. They then took me on board a brig belonging to the port, and the captain agreed to give me twenty dollars per month to go with him as cook and cabin boy, advancing me one month's pay to furnish myself with clothes and other things I needed or wanted.

Our first voyage was to Havre de Grace [Le Havre?]where we arrived after a passage of forty days. While we were there, the captain had to go to Paris, where he remained for more than a fortnight. During his absence, I heard that an American merchantman, the *Grand Turk*, belonging to Boston, was bound for London. I felt a strong desire to return to England so I went to her captain and he agreed that I should go with him in the same situation I had just left for twelve dollars a month. He promised that, if I deserved more, he would give it to me.

To my great disappointment, we did not go to London but to Copenhagen, which took fourteen days. When we arrived the captain discharged all the crew except the mate and myself. He took on a new crew, consisting entirely of Danes, and passed himself off as supercargo, the first mate as passenger, and myself as a servant to both. He was very generous, advancing my wages to fifteen dollars per month, and putting me before the mast [ie making Rattenbury an apprentice seaman]. He praised my diligence and activity, and assured me that while I was with him, if I continued to act as hitherto, I would never want for a friend.

We sailed for Gothenburg where we remained five weeks, taking in a cargo of hemp, iron, potash and soap. We were proceeding with it to Havre de Grace when we were driven into a creek near Crushing Sands [Kristiansand?] in Norway, where we had to stay for three months because of the weather. When the wind became fair we resumed our voyage and arrived safe at Havre de Grace in ten days.

We discharged our cargo and the supercargo, who told me he was going as a passenger to America, paid me off. He gave me a very handsome letter of recommendation and we parted with mutual regret. He paid me in French paper-money, but I could not get it changed. At a loss to know what to do with it, I decided to lay it out in clothes and fiddles [trifles?] with a view to disposing of them in barter at the first opportunity.

Through the recommendation I obtained a situation with another American captain, and as the supercargo had given me a very high character, he agreed to advance my pay to sixteen dollars per month. We took in our cargo of wine and proceeded on our voyage. Our destination was unknown because the captain did not make it public, but after five days sailing we arrived safe at Guernsey. There I sold my clothes and fiddles. There too, to my great joy, I met my uncle. He had come over with bullocks for the English troops stationed there.

When we had discharged our cargo, I applied to our captain for leave to go home. He readily consented, but on the condition that I return to him when the time specified for my leave of absence had expired. I agreed, and went aboard the vessel with my uncle.

In two days I arrived safe at Beer and there had the pleasure of seeing my mother, and my childhood friends. They were overjoyed to see me, and I told them of the adventures I had met with.

Also back at Beer were some of my old shipmates from the prison at Bordeaux who had been released and had found their way back to England. They were all interested in what had occurred during the period of our separation.

According to Rattenbury, he was absent from home for two years. For most of that time no-one in Beer, or in the prison in Bordeaux, can have known what had happened to him. Anne Raddenbury must have thought that, like his father, he would never return. but he did, probably in the summer of 1795, a year after Reverend Swete's visit. He would have been sixteen years old.

CHANNEL PORTS

CHAPTER 3

Fisherman, Smuggler and Seaman
1795-1798

Working as a seaman on vessels transporting goods around European ports, and to America, taught young Rattenbury a great deal about the mercantile trade. What the master of the American merchantman gained by taking on a Danish crew and passing himself off as supercargo is unclear, but the most likely explanation is that diluting the vessel's American identity helped protect it in encounters with English privateers.

Socially, the world of the 18th Century seafarer have been quite small, therefore Rattenbury meeting his uncle on Guernsey was not an exceptional circumstance, particularly as Seaton and Beer merchants had strong business links with those of the Channel Islands.

Guernsey and Alderney play such an important part in Rattenbury's story that it is worthwhile pausing here to look at the privileged status enjoyed by them at this time. Closer to the French coast than the English, the Channel Islanders' centuries-old loyalty to the Crown had been rewarded by being allowed to retain many of their own customs and laws, one of which was that their ports should remain Free. Not subject to the revenue laws of Britain, the foreign goods purchased there did not carry British taxes unless, or until, they were imported into Britain. Thus the Islands became a convenient place for merchants to purchase such goods, and for those who also intended to smuggle them.

So brisk did this trade become that warehouses sprung up on the Islands to cater specifically for it. Here French traders could deposit their goods for the English to buy, even when their two countries were at war, which they were almost constantly throughout the 18th Century. In fact, it was to pay for those wars that the British government kept slapping ever higher duties on imported goods, notably spirits and tobacco.

The price of a gallon of brandy purchased in France or the Channel Islands was four shillings; the same gallon purchased legally in England could be as much as 34 shillings. Who was going to pay 34 shillings for a product if it was available at eleven or twelve shillings? Very few people indeed, therefore a booming market was created for contraband goods, a market readily and eagerly addressed by smuggling entrepreneurs. Even allowing for transportation costs, and the loss of cargos to storm, customs seizures, or bribes, the smuggler could seriously undercut the prices of legal importers and still make a handsome profit.

These entrepreneurs bought their goods from the Channel Islands, and the Channel Islands grew wealthy on the proceeds. On Guernsey and Alderney in the late 18th and early 19th Centuries, brandy and gin were prepared for smuggling, being sold in waterproof tubs, slung together with ropes, ready for sinking as rafts in the sea off the coast of England! According to J R W Coxhead in *Smuggling Days in Devon*, some Guernsey Islanders made fortunes by manufacturing casks alone. Demand for storage space was so great that the island's huge system of underground vaults and cellars was inadequate for the task.

The Channel Islands were not only ideally placed to take advantage of the smuggling trade, but that of privateering too. About 300 ships, barques, brigs and schooners were built in Guernsey's shipyards in the hundred years preceding Rattenbury's visit, and many of them were involved in privateering. It was not unusual for a Guernsey vessel, operating under a Letter of Marque in order to help the British government in its war against the French, to be actively involved in the smuggling trade which cheated that same government out of the revenue needed to wage it!

So active were the Islanders as privateers that in the year of Rattenbury's birth (1778), when the French were supporting the Americans in their War of Independence, the Governor of Cherbourg is reported to have said that the Islands 'are the despair of France at the breaking out of each war, through their remarkably active privateers. The habit of encountering the dangers of the sea renders the natives very brave'.

At the close of that war, with the signing of the Treaty of Versailles in 1783, the total worth of the prizes taken by Guernsey privateers amounted to £900,000. In 1794 alone - the year before Rattenbury's visit - seven prizes were taken into St Peter Port, Guernsey's main harbour.

It would have been in St Peter Port that John Rattenbury met his uncle. The building of Fort George, just to the south of the town, was begun in 1782, since when a battalion of the English regular army had been stationed there. It was probably to supply these soldiers that Rattenbury's uncle had brought the bullocks. His visit, coinciding with young Rattenbury's arrival, meant that the well-travelled youth could go back to Beer at last.

There is every likelihood that, on the homeward voyage aboard his uncle's vessel, John Rattenbury was accompanied by a cargo of contraband because, in 1795, some Beer and Seaton merchants and smugglers were in either in partnership with the merchant-smugglers of Alderney, connections which may have developed in the 1760s when the Beer Gang was active.

There is little doubt that in the 1770s some Alderney merchants

5. Weymouth Custom House. Home of the Robilliard family 1795-1810

were running contraband into Weymouth. In support of this view, an important piece of evidence came to light in 1885, while part of the *George Inn* was being dismantled. In a wall crevice was found a piece of paper. It was dated 24 April 1776 and on it was written an account made out for eight casks of brandy at 16/6 each, seven casks of rum at 15/6 each, a flagon of brandy and a flagon of rum at 11 shillings, and 24 pounds of tea, all received from Peter le Coq by W Matthew. The total bill was £14.5.0d and it the money was paid on 17

September to Thomas Martin, Peter le Coq's representative. It is obvious from the concealment of the account, and the prices quoted, that the transaction was in smuggled goods.

According to shipping registers, Peter le Coq, or le Cocq, was an Alderney merchant. (The le Cocqs were a notable Alderney family, and in 1738 a Thomas le Cocq was suspended from exercising his functions as an Alderney judge on account of 'alleged irregularities'). A Peter le Cocq was smuggling in 1776, and a Peter le Cocq was smuggling sixteen years later in 1792 when, along with fellow Alderney merchants Thomas Nicholas Robilliard, and John and William Sandford, he became the owner of the cutter *Lively*, built in Mevagissey, Cornwall. Her captain was Robert Chiles.

The Robilliards had strong Weymouth connections. On the quay is a house which is presently used as offices by HM Coastguard. In 1874 it was the Custom House. However, between 1794 and 1810 it was a warehouse belonging to two Channel Island merchants - Ahier and Robilliard. The Robilliard family actually lived on the premises, residing on the lower floor. Ahier and Robilliard went out of business in 1810, which coincides with the decline in Channel Island smuggling due to the establishment of customs outports on Guernsey and Jersey in 1807.

Between 1790 and 1808, however, the market was still strong and it was during this period that the names of Robilliard, Chiles and Sandford appear again and again in connection with vessels which, like the *Lively,* were either suspected by Customs of transporting contraband, or actually seized and condemned for doing so. As the ownership of some of these same vessels was shared with the merchants and mariners of Seaton and Beer, the smuggling connection between the two communities cannot be ignored. The arrival of a Beer boat in Guernsey in 1795 was not in the least bit unusual. It was his uncle who took Rattenbury home, but it could just as easily have been another local mariner.

I was now about sixteen years of age. After all my vicissitudes on a restless sea, I hankered after some ease and therefore abandoned all thoughts of returning to Guernsey. I forfeited my promise to the American captain. This was wrong because the engagement was a voluntary act and should have been fulfilled.

I remained at home about six months, part of that time occupied in fishing. After the roving life I had left, this employment seemed dull and tiresome so, as the smuggling trade was then being plied very briskly in the neighbourhood, I decided to try my fortune in it, and engaged in a small vessel which sailed out of Lyme to the Islands [Channel Islands]. The voyage was quite successful, but within four months the vessel was laid up and I was again in want of a situation.

Rattenbury implies that he was in the Beer area for less than a year, but it must have been much longer - two years at least, probably three, ie between 1795 and March 1798. He says he fished, and he smuggled, but smuggled for whom? A letter written to the Customs Board in London on 26 October 1795 by the collector at Exeter, cites some possibilities:

> "Respecting the present state of smuggling within this district, there does not appear to have been any increase on that article within the last two years. On the contrary it has rather been on the decrease for several years past.
>
> The trade within this Port is at present chiefly confined to the smugglers residing at Beer and Seaton, about twenty miles to the east of this city, in the vessels mentioned on the back hereof, which are mostly owned by the smugglers themselves. These vessels make about six or eight trips a year, and bring in generally from 100-200 kegs containing from 2-6 gallons each of brandy, rum and geneva [gin], a few bags of manufactured tobacco, and some small bags of black tea, each trip.
>
> They seldom... come within the limits prescribed by law with their cargos on board, but have large boats belonging to them into which they put the goods about mid-Channel. As opportunity serves, they land them to the eastward or westward of this harbour in a small creek, unless they are informed by signals from the shore that the Revenue Officers are on the look-out, when they sink them as rafts about 2-3 miles off the land. At a future time, they take them up with small boats and send part on shore at one creek, and part at another, at which time they have spies placed on the hills and cliffs along the coast to give notice by lighting one, two, or three fires, at what creek, or creeks, the Revenue Officers are stationed. They then proceed to another creek and are met by their friends from the shore, who are provided with horses, and the goods are immediately dispersed through the country." (PRO. Exeter Letterbooks CUST 64/11)

The names of the smuggling vessels - *Mayflower, Dove, Experiment, Ranger, Fanny, Mary,* and the Lyme-registered *Hawke* - were written on the back of the letter, as were the names of their owners and masters. Some owners, or part-owners, were masters of their own vessels, some master of another. The names included John Violett (Seaton merchant and victualler), Daniel French (Beer mariner), Thomas and William Wills, John Searle, William Marshall, Jonathan Miller, and a Robilliard.

Hawke had been registered at Lyme on 5 October 1792 when her master was John Chamberlain of Seaton. Peter Gibbs of Beer, who took over in 1794, was the master when she was named in the report.

Was *Hawke* the Lyme vessel John Rattenbury said he went smuggling in?

Other contemporary sources point accusing fingers not just at Violett and French, but at Beer and Seaton residents not mentioned in the report, the most notable being John and William Head (Seaton wine merchants), and Thomas Bidney. The masters with the best smuggling 'form' were Peter Gibbs of Beer, John Searle, John Newton, Thomas Cookney Jnr, Bartholomew Wesley (or Westlake?), and Joseph Bishop of Lyme. The Wills family were part-owners of the *Mary* with a Robilliard, and a John Robilliard acquired a share in John Violett's square-sterned cutter *Mayflower*. John and William Head were also associates of the Robilliards. In 1797, with Thomas Robilliard, they owned the *Friends Goodwill*, which was transferred to Guernsey in May 1798.

In 1795 Rattenbury's uncle, operating out of Beer, was supplying bullocks to the English army in Guernsey. Was he working for Violett the victualler? Was it John Newton?

John Newton was often employed as a master by John and William Head. He commanded their *John Edward* in 1789 and their *Brilliant* in April 1791. In August 1793 he was in charge of the *Dundas* owned by Lyme mariner John Urquart. In November 1795, he captained the *Mary*, owned by Seaton and Beer mariner Richard Raddon, then in September 1797 it was *Brothers*, owned by Daniel French, Thomas Wills and Thomas Bidney. There is no doubt that John Newton smuggled. Both Urquart's *Dundas* and Daniel French's *Brothers* were seized by customs while he was in charge of them. *Dundas* was such a good vessel, and so fast, that in November 1795 she was taken into the revenue service at Cowes where she shared privateering and anti-smuggling duties with another former smuggling vessel, *Nancy*. Oddly enough, it is *Nancy* which features strongly in the next part of John Rattenbury's story, not *Dundas*.

It is now March 1798. Rattenbury is nineteen years old and looking for employment.

> I applied to Captain Jarvis, and agreed to go on a voyage with him in a vessel called the *Friends*, which belonged to Beer and Seaton, but which was then lying in Bridport harbour.
>
> As soon as she was rigged we went to sea, but contrary winds came on and we were obliged to put into Lyme. The next day the wind was favourable so, at 6 o'clock in the evening, we put to sea again, and proceeded to Tenby in Wales, where we were bound for culm.

The vessel *Friends* was a brig built at Lyme and registered there on 26 June 1796. On 20 November 1797, she was re-registered in London. Her master was Thomas Jarvis.

Rattenbury says that *Friends* was bound for Tenby for culm. Culm, although regarded officially as coal-mining waste, was in fact small pieces of coal, no more than about 2" in diameter. In Devon it was purchased to fire kilns for burning limestone from which lime was extracted for agricultural and building use. We don't know whether *Friends* really was going to Wales, but we do know she sailed from Lyme on 16 March 1798.

> At 8 o'clock the captain set the watch, and it was my turn to remain below. At twelve I went on deck and was there until four, when I went below again. I had scarcely dropped off the sleep when I was aroused by hearing the captain exclaim "Come on deck, my good fellow! Here is a privateer, and we shall all be taken."
> I got up and found the privateer close alongside of us. Its captain hailed us in English. He asked what port we were from, and where we were bound. Our captain told the truth. Their captain then sent a boat with an officer in her. He took on board his own vessel all hands, except myself and a little boy who had never been to sea before, and sent his prize-master and four men aboard our brig. Their orders were to take her into the nearest French port.

It was customary for a privateer captain to take the crew of a captured vessel on board his own ship, replacing them with a skeleton crew of his own, under a prize-master. The prize-master's duty was to take the prize back to the home port with all possible speed, thus leaving the privateer free to continue cruising in the hope of capturing more prizes.

> When the privateer had gone, the prize-master ordered me to go aloft and loose the main top-gallant sail, which I did. When I came down I noticed that, through ignorance of the coast, he was steering very wildly. I offered to take the helm and he let me. He directed me to steer south-east by south, and then went below where he was soon drinking and carousing with his companions. Occasionally they sent me up a glass of grog, and these so animated my spirits that I began to think I might not only escape, but be revenged on them.
> A fog came up, which aided my design, and I altered course to east by north, in the hope that we would fall in with an English vessel. As the day advanced, the fog dispersed, and the sky became clear enough for us to see land. The prize-master and his companions asked me what land it was.
> "Alderney," I said, and they believed me, although at the time we were just off the island of Portland!
> We hauled our wind more to the south until we cleared Portland Bill. We soon came within sight of the land at St. Alban's Head [Dorset]. The prize-master asked again what land it was we could see.
> "Cape La Hogue," I said.

My companions then became suspicious and angry. They took our captain's dog, threw him overboard, and knocked down his house, as though to intimate that my fate would be the same if I was deceiving them.

When we were within a league of Swanage, I persuaded them to go on shore to get a pilot. They hoisted out a boat, and I got into it with them. I was very apprehensive about the outcome of all this, but hope animated me, and my fortunate genius urged me on.

When we were close to shore, the people there hailed us - in English of course - and told us to keep further west. My companions now began to swear, and said the people were speaking English. I denied this, and urged them to hail again. As they were rising to do so, I plunged overboard.

I came up the other side of the boat and they struck at me with their oars. They snapped a pistol at me, but it misfired. I went on swimming. Every time they attempted to strike me, I made a dive and disappeared. Their boat started to take in water, and finding that their pursuit of me was not only vain but endangering themselves, they turned round and rowed away as fast as possible back to the vessel.

Having got rid of my foes, I strove for the shore, which I reached only with great difficulty. The men in the boat had reached the brig and, spreading all their canvasses, bore away for the French coast. I was afraid they would get away with the vessel so I sent two men for assistance, one to the signal-house at St. Alban's, and another to Swanage. Fortunately, in Swanage Bay at that time was a small cutter belonging to His Majesty's Customs. She was called the *Nancy* and was commanded by Captain Willis.

As soon as he had received the information, he made all sail after them. I was not on board because I did not reach them in time, which was disappointing, but apparently the cutter came up with the brig about 9 o'clock in the evening and she was retaken. She was taken into Cowes the same night and there the men who had been on board were put in prison.

The *Nancy* was a small cutter of 34 tons which had been in the service of the customs at Cowes since March 1796. Her captain was Robert Willis. She had been a smuggling vessel used by the Wernham Brothers of Hastings but because of her speed, William Arnold, the collector at Cowes, fitted her out as a temporary revenue cruiser. She came into her own after 14 December 1796 when Arnold's chief revenue cutter, the newly built *Swan III*, was lost to a French privateer. Captain Sarman and several of his crew were killed in that engagement, the rest captured and imprisoned at Roquefort from which they were not released until nine months later. *Nancy* carried out *Swan III*'s duties while *Swan IV* was being built at Cowes.

Nancy was a fine little vessel and Willis was an able commander. Together they scored notable successes against French privateers -

6. Swan *attacked by French luggers off the Needles*

capturing the *Daphne* of Cherbourg (formerly the *Vigilant* privateer of Guernsey) in March 1797 - and against smugglers. In the recapture of the *Friends* Willis may have scored a success on both fronts for he rescued from a privateer what William Arnold believed was a smuggling vessel. This is made clear on 20 March 1798 in Arnold's letter to the Customs Board:

> *"We beg leave to acquaint you for the Honorable Board's information that Mr Robert Willis, Commander of the* Nancy *Revenue Cutter of this Port, has retaken and brought in an English Brig in Ballast called the* Friends *of London, which had been taken on the Morning of the 17th Inst, about five or six leagues to the Westward of Portland by a French Privateer of Cherburgh called* Heureux Speculatieur, *Louis Ben Mathias Morgueror(?), Commander.*
>
> *By an English Lad who was on Board the Retaken Brig, we are informed that she sailed from Lyme the Evening before she was taken and was bound for Tenby for Coals, and he adds that Philip Head of Seaton and Daniel French of Beer were owners of the Brig, though she sailed as of London and is marked in the stern*

Friends of London, *which induces us to suspect that the vessel was in fact bound for Guernsey or Alderney on the smuggling Trade.*" (PRO. Cowes Letterbooks CUST 61/135)

This account tallies well with Rattenbury's, although the source of the information was different, the 'English lad' being the 'little boy who had never been to sea before'.

Arnold suspected that *Friends* was on a smuggling trip, and given that the owners were Daniel French and a member of the Head family of Seaton, his suspicions seem fully justified! On that same day, Arnold wrote to his opposite number at Lyme, informing him of the brig's recapture and asking for confirmation of the vessel's ownership, as no register or other papers had been found on board at the time of her recapture. Rattenbury also mentions a letter:

> Captain Willis sent me a letter stating what he had done, and advising me to go as quickly as possible to the owners to inform them of what had taken place. This I did and one of them immediately set off for Cowes, getting the vessel back by paying salvage.
>
> The transaction over, I was elated at the part I had taken, but I never received any reward for the service I had rendered, either from the owners, or from any other quarter. The affair was much talked of at the time, and an account of it was inserted in the public papers.
>
> The owners appointed another captain to replace the one who had been taken to France as a prisoner. I went with them to Cowes and rejoined the brig. Two days later, a lieutenant and his gang [press gang] paid us a visit with a view to impressing men. When it came to my turn to be examined, I told him that I was an apprentice by the name of German Phillips, a young man whose indenture I kept for protection. This stratagem was to no avail with the keen-eyed lieutenant, and he immediately took me aboard the guard ship, the *Royal William*, then lying at Spithead. There I remained in close confinement for a month, hoping that I might find a way to make my escape, but with no prospect of success, I volunteered my service for the Royal Navy.

The Admiralty's Impress Service was a large scale organisation with officers and places of rendezvous in many key ports and towns throughout the country. An Impress Boat and four men were stationed at Cowes in 1795 and it seems that they were still active three years later in March 1798 when Rattenbury was swept into their net.

In readiness for their work, the officers of the Impress Service not only kept a large supply of warrants, but had at their disposal guard ships like the *Royal William*, in which impressed seamen were confined, sometimes in squalid and unhealthy conditions until, like Rattenbury, they 'volunteered' to serve.

Customs sometimes assisted the Admiralty in its impressment work, but the two services did not always see eye to eye, particularly as the finest seamen available to the gangs were, of course, those employed on board revenue cruisers! In June 1795, an officer belonging to the *Swan* cutter of Cowes was bringing in a small smuggling lugger laden with foreign spirits and other goods when, between Spithead and Cowes, it was boarded by a naval officer and eight of his men, The revenue officer was accused of being a smuggler and threatened with the same guard ship *Royal William*, again at Spithead, but he managed to convince the naval officer that he was a revenue officer. The sailors left, but returned almost immediately and took by force 15-20 casks of spirits, cutting adrift the revenue boat to prevent a pursuit. In a letter to Lord Bridport, commander of the naval forces at Spithead, William Arnold complained bitterly about the conduct of the naval officer and his men

Rattenbury also had strong views about press gangs. As a seaman he was always at risk from them and, given that the navy had deprived him of his father, he was entitled to be passionate about impressment:

> Can it be called a voluntary act when it is the result of necessity and not inclination? Impressing seamen is a common practice in the time of war, yet our country is called the land of liberty? We possess a just and invincible aversion to slavery at home and in our foreign colonies - it is stated triumphantly that a slave cannot breathe in England - yet how is this to be reconciled with the practice of tearing men from the weeping and afflicted families, from the peaceable and useful pursuits of merchandise and commerce, and chaining them to a situation which is repugnant to their feelings and their principles? On the day of battle, an impressed seaman may sacrifice his resentment on the altar of patriotism or, inspired by the example of others, he may perform miracles of valour, but his ordinary duties he finds intolerably irksome, and is therefore ready to seize any opportunity to regain his liberty.

Are these the words of John Rattenbury, illiterate smuggler, or of J Harvey, printer?

> As soon as I had agreed to enter the service, I was put on board a cutter, and went on a cruise off the islands of Guernsey, Alderney etc, for a fortnight, after which we returned to Spithead.
>
> Soon after our arrival there, I went on shore with the lieutenant and some of the crew. There I met my old master from Brixham. As he was going to sail for Brixham the following morning, he took me on board his fishing smack. A day later he put me on shore at Portland so that I might be nearer home. Too late, I recollected that I had left my pocket-book behind on the cutter.

I went home quickly cautiously, exchanging with a young man the cap I wore for his hat. I avoided Lyme because I knew a gang was always kept there. I did not meet any interruption and, after a very fatiguing walk, got to Beer.

I had been home about a week when some of the men from the cutter came to Lyme in search of me. By means of my pocket book, the lieutenant had discovered my real name, and that I was not German Phillips as on the indenture. On their way they laid hold of the young man who had my cap because they knew it belonged to German Phillips, but they soon realised he was not the person they were looking for. After various enquiries - all unsuccessful - they relinquished the pursuit and went back to Portsmouth.

The indenture held by Rattenbury was designed to keep him out of naval service, apprentices being exempt from impressment, but was it a stolen document or a forgery? We don't know. We do know, however, that on 14 January 1798, only a few months before the events described in this chapter took place, the Beer and Seaton parish register records the baptism of Germin Philips, son of Giles and Judith Philips.

NORTH ATLANTIC

Waterford

Bee

Porto

Madeira

The Azores

Newfoundland

New York

CHAPTER 4

Ireland, Newfoundland, and Captivity in Spain
1798-1800

Rattenbury, in recalling past events for his *Memoirs*, was not always accurate about the year they occurred. He gives a date of 1800 for many of the events in this chapter, when documentary evidence places them firmly in the previous year. For this edition, his account has been amended.

> The next six months I spent fishing and smuggling, but I had no great inclination for either employment. About this time the gang [press gang] at Lyme broke up, so I went there and worked in the coasting and victualling trade until the beginning of 1799.
>
> In February 1799, having been informed that a brig lying at Topsham required hands, I went to see the captain, whose name was Elson, and agreed to go with him for £4 10s per month. By the end of March our vessel was ready for sea, and having a fair wind, we proceeded on our voyage.

The vessel was the *Bickford*, a square-sterned brigantine owned by Topsham merchant James Jackson, and William Bickford Jackson of Bideford. The master was Henry Elson Jnr.

> We put into Waterford for provisions but, soon after our departure, the vessel sprung a leak and we had to go back and take out all our stores in order to get it repaired. Lord Rolle, who was in that part of Ireland with his regiment at the time, kindly sent seventeen of his soldiers to assist us, thereby lightening our labour and accelerating the completion of our task.

Lord John Rolle (1750-1842), of Stevenstone, Great Torrington, Devon, was several times MP for Devon. He owned Bicton House, East Budleigh, about nine miles from Beer, and through his marriage to Judith Maria Walrond in 1773, had also acquired Bovey House, just outside Beer. For many years he commanded the South Devon Militia which, according to an item in the *Exeter Flying Post*, returned from duty in Ireland in July 1799 so it must have been in March 1799 that Lord Rolle rendered Captain Elson and his crew such a valuable service in Waterford.

The leak being stopped we put to sea again, and after a three-week passage, arrived at St. John's, the principal port of Newfoundland. There we landed our passengers, and part of our cargo, before proceeding around Cape St. Mary to Placentia, where we discharged another part. We discharged the remainder at Pacee [Trespassey] where our vessel was laid up. We stayed at Newfoundland three months, during which time we were busy, and successful, taking and curing cod.

NEWFOUNDLAND

Newfoundland's fishing grounds had been controlled by English merchants since the 16th Century. Shiploads of fish were regularly transported to markets in southern Europe, particularly Portugal. The earliest European inhabitants of Newfoundland were itinerant employees working for the fish merchants, and most were from the south west coast of England, the link with Devon being particularly strong. It was not until the late 17th Century that the workers became settlers, staying long enough to start bringing up families. At the time of Rattenbury's visit, a succession of English naval officers had acted as the island's governors, there being no regular governor - because there had been no regular settlement - until 1817.

Our arrangements being completed in November, we left that bleak spot and went to sea again, with a cargo of prime fish, bound for Oporto [Porto, Portugal], where we intended to dispose of it. When we were about four leagues from our destination, we had the misfortune to fall in with a Spanish privateer, which chased us. At 10 o'clock the next morning, she came up to us and we were obliged to lie-to. Her captain then sent some of his people alongside our vessel to take off all the crew except myself and an Irish lad. He sent a prize-master and ten men on board, and their instructions were to take our brig into Vigo, to which port the privateer belonged.

While in this situation, I kept thinking of schemes for getting the upper-hand of the enemy, and I might have managed it several times, had the Irish youth been sufficiently alert to the hints I gave. But my efforts were fruitless, so I endeavoured to make myself as useful as I could to the Spanish officer managing the vessel.

We arrived at Vigo in December. The prize-master was so pleased with my behaviour that, when we came ashore, he took me to his own house to live with him. He recommended me in such strong terms to the owner of the privateer, that I was presented with thirty dollars, given my liberty, and lent a mule to take me to Vienna [Viana do Castelo?].

In Vienna [Viana do Castelo?] I went to see the British consul who told me that if I asked for assistance he would detain me till some English man-of-war arrived [ie the consul threatened to impress Rattenbury], so I simply asked for a pass. This he granted and I went on to Oporto, travelling through a district abounding with the finest landscapes. However, I was so depressed by my misfortunes, and so intent on getting home, that I could not appreciate fully the beauties of the surrounding country.

When I reached Oporto, I applied to the English consul for assistance. He was a kind-hearted man, and after I had given him my pass and shown him the recommendation of the Spanish prize-master, he very humanely appointed me a house where I was to be boarded free of expense until I could find some means of returning to England.

I had been in Oporto a few days when, recovered from my fatiguing journey, I went down on the quay to look out for a ship. As soon as I got there, I was hailed from a vessel by someone I knew. I went on board and, to my great joy, found my late captain and shipmates on the deck. Our surprise was mutual, and after our emotions subsided, they explained that when the captain of the Spanish privateer arrived at the port, he had generously given them their liberty, and put them aboard the Danish brig on which I now found them.

41

We spent a very pleasant hour together, then we all went on shore where I introduced them to the English consul. He received them kindly, and gave them leave to go to the house where I was stationed, where they could stay until they too had an opportunity to return home.

Vigo in Spain is eighty miles from Porto in Portugal. As Vienna is 1500 miles from both it is extremely unlikely that Rattenbury travelled by mule from one to the other via Austria! It is much more likely that he went to Viana do Castelo, a coastal town midway between Vigo and Oporto.

That same evening, I went down to the quay alone, and was delighted to find lying there a schooner bound for Guernsey. I made enquiries about the name of the merchant to whom she belonged, went to see him, and told him my story. He said that, although he could not engage me properly, if I went on board and assisted in loading the vessel, he would satisfy me for my time, and a proper agreement might result. I followed his advice and the vessel was soon laden with oranges, lemons, and other fruits belonging to the country. The captain returned, and when I told him what had passed between the merchant and myself, and showed him the character I had received from the Spanish prize-master, he agreed to take me with him as his mate.

We put to sea and had fine weather for the first few days, but then heavy gales of wind came on. They so damaged the vessel that we were compelled to bear away for the coast of Ireland. Off Cape Clear, we fell in with an Indiaman's mast and rigging, but could not cut anything away because we had on board no tools but a blunt old axe.

When the weather cleared up, we saw a frigate about a mile ahead of us. It was the *Naiad*, and its captain sent a boat alongside us to discover what wreck we had fallen in with. On being told what it was, he sent to our assistance his carpenter, who took the mast for firewood, leaving us with the rigging. We put into Glendower in Ireland, and thence proceeded to Baltimore [Ireland], where we got a note of protest [a written declaration made by the master of a ship, and signed by a magistrate, stating the circumstances in which a ship, or its cargo, had been damaged], and had the vessel repaired.

As soon as the weather became calmer, we ventured to sea, but we were out for only three days when tremendous gales came on again. We were driven about by the tumultuous elements, in imminent peril of our lives, and it was only with difficulty that we reached the Cove of Cork.

We remained at Cork for several days, then the weather being fairer, we recommenced our voyage. We were at sea five or six days with the wind in our favour when, just as we came off the Lizard Point, it changed to south-east, obliging us to go into Mount's Bay. There the captain sold the rigging wc had salvaged and shared the money amongst us, which proved useful as we were in need of many things.

We remained in Mount's Bay for a week, then sailed for Guernsey, where we landed on 25 March [1800]. There the captain sold the schooner, and having taken a brig belonging to his brother-in-law, pressed me kindly to be his mate. I declined for I had discovered that there was a Weymouth packet lying at Guernsey and it was on the point of sailing. I went on her as a passenger and arrived safe at Beer the following day. I had been absent for rather more than twelve months.

The Post Office had started running a regular packet from Guernsey to Weymouth and back in 1794. Their two ships were the 80-ton *Chesterfield*, and the *Rover*, which came from Dover where the regular postal service had been suspended at the outbreak of war with France in 1793. It was probably on one of these two vessels that Rattenbury sailed to Weymouth.

CHAPTER 5

Marriage; privateering aboard the *Alert*
1800

> Before I set out on my last voyage, I had fixed my affections on a young woman in the neighbourhood, and it was agreed that our union should take place as soon as I returned. I claimed the fulfillment of this promise, and we were married on 17 April 1800.

In the 1837 edition of the *Memoirs*, it is stated that he was married on 17 April 1801, but the parish register at Lyme gives the date as 17 April 1800.

Prior to his voyage to Newfoundland, Rattenbury had been living in Lyme, and it was there he met Anna Partridge, the daughter of Abraham and Frances Partridge (nee Nichols). Unusually, Anna was nine years old when she was baptised in 1791, and would therefore have been about eighteen when she married. Rattenbury was twenty-one. They probably met through a seafaring connection - in 1792 an Abraham Partridge is recorded as having been the master of the *Wren* of Lyme.

In the 18th and early 19th Century, the spelling of names was erratic to say the least. Many versions can exist even the same individual is being referred to. 'Anna Partridge' is a good example. Anna's Christian name has been transcribed as Ann and Hannah, and her surname is sometimes recorded as Patridge. The entry for their marriage refers to John Rottenbury of Lyme Regis, bachelor, and Hannah Partridge of the same parish, spinster, who signed her own as Anna! Rattenbury was illiterate.

There were Partridges in Beer, but as the distance from Lyme is less than seven miles, that is hardly to be wondered at. However the Lyme Rottonbery families (transcribed as Rottinbury, Rottingbery, Rotenbury etc.) do not appear to have been closely related to John Rattenbury. Their link with the Raddenburys of Honiton may have been equally as tenuous.

> We resided at Lyme, but as I could not obtain regular employment, I decided to go privateering again. I was accordingly engaged by Captain Diamond to go with him aboard the *Alert*, a Weymouth lugger, then at Bridport being fitted out for the purpose. We completed our stores and, in May, set sail for Alderney, where we took in our stock and wine and spirits. We then steered to the Western Islands [the Azores] on a cruise, hoping to encounter Spanish vessels.

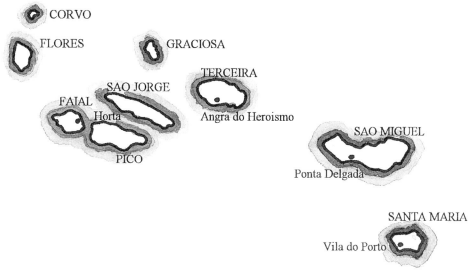

CORVO

FLORES

GRACIOSA

TERCEIRA

SAO JORGE

FAIAL

Horta

Angra do Heroismo

SAO MIGUEL

PICO

Ponta Delgada

SANTA MARIA

Vila do Porto

The AZORES

The 117-ton *Alert* sailed from Weymouth with a crew of 45 soon after 28 April 1800, which is when she was awarded her Letter of Marque. She had been registered there on 22 April by customs, who recorded that in their port at the time there were 55 ships and 172 seamen employed in the coasting trade, 25 vessels and 77 fishermen in the fishing trade, and four ships and 77 British seamen in the foreign trade.

The *Alert* was a brand new lugger built by Nicholas Bools and William Good of Bridport for John and Joseph Horsford, John Kocart and linen draper James Scott, all of Weymouth. Her captain was Thomas Diamond. Her owners must have hoped she would encounter Spanish vessels conveying the produce of the Americas back to Spain for they sent her on a cruise to the North Atlantic.

> We were at sea for three months, and then put in at St Michael's [Sao Miguel, in the Azores]. There, in the roads, we found a large ship from Rio de la Plata [River Plate], laden with hides and tallow. We tried

various manoeuvres to entice her out, but without success. As it was a neutral port, we were obliged to put to sea again and leave her behind.

That same day, we fell in with the *Concord* frigate and our captain went on board. When he mentioned our recent circumstances, he was informed that there was another ship from the Rio de la Plata at Faial [another island in the Azores]. He went in to measure the distance, but found that we were within the limits.

For some days we kept in company with the frigate, but were parted during the night. After cruising for some time, we went into Faial to look for the Spanish ship which the *Concord*'s captain had told us about. She was there all right and we tried everything in our power to decoy her out, but our stratagems were ineffective and we had to withdraw. We put into Port-a-Pin [?] close by, went on shore, and drank with the Spaniards. The boatswain and four others agreed to enter on board our vessel, which they did, but when they got back to shore they were found out, and taken prisoners.

It appears that the English privateer crew enlisted the help of some of the Spanish vessel's crew - probably with promises of a share in the prize money - to help capture their own ship! The plot was discovered and the traitors confined. The commander of the Spanish ship was displeased:

A few days later we went in again. Our captain spoke to the consul who advised us to make off as quickly as possible because he suspected that the Spaniards intended to fire on us. We took his advice and went on another cruise.

On our return we put into St. Ubes [Setubal?] in Portugal, to replenish our stock of provisions. The captain asked us if we would go to sea again for one month and, on his promising to give us a month's wages in advance, we agreed.

After being quarantined at St. Ubes, we left the port and continued cruising, without success, until Christmas Day. The captain mustered all hands and asked us if we wanted to abandon the undertaking and return to England? We said yes so, putting the helm hard-a-weather, we steered for home.

On the way, we encountered the *Alert*, a King's cutter and our captain went on board. The principal officer threatened to impress us all, but our captain said that we were such resolute and desperate fellows that if he attempted any such thing we would blow him and his vessel out of the water. When our captain returned, and we heard what had taken place, we immediately put him below and took charge of the vessel ourselves, hoisting all the sail we could. We got safe into Weymouth on Sunday 28 December 1800, and I went immediately to see my wife at Lyme.

Captain Thomas Diamond must have been relieved of command soon after the *Alert* arrived in Weymouth because on 16 January 1801, it is reported as having a new master in Thomas Chiles. Diamond appears in the Lyme shipping register again in December 1807 as the master of *True Briton*, a former prize vessel purchased by a co-operative of about 25 merchants, including members of the Downe family of Bridport, and the Head family of Seaton.

CHAPTER 6

Living in Lyme;
trouble with the Press Gang
1801-1805

After returning to Weymouth on the *Alert*, Rattenbury went home to Anna in Lyme. It was 1801 and Lyme was not just a busy port offering employment to a sailor like Rattenbury, but was increasingly popular with summer visitors. One of them was novelist Jane Austen who, in September 1804, spent a holiday there with members of her family. She liked the town and used it as the setting for an important section of her novel *Persuasion*, first published in 1818. She had Captain Wentworth's party visiting out of season:

> "They were come too late in the year for any amusement or variety which Lyme, as a public place, might offer; the rooms were shut up, the lodgers almost all gone, scarcely any family but of the residents left - and, as there is nothing to admire in the buildings themselves, the remarkable situation of the town, the principal street almost hurrying into the water, the walk to the Cobb, skirting round the pleasant little bay, which in the season is animated with bathing machines and company, the Cobb itself, its old wonder and new improvements, with the very beautiful line of cliffs stretching out to the east of the town, are what the stranger's eye will seek; and a very strange stranger it must be, who does not see charms in the immediate environs of Lyme, to make him wish to know it better."

At the time of Jane Austen's visit in 1804, John Rattenbury and his family were residents, and it is interesting to conjecture whether some of the Downe family of nearby Bridport were there too - in a letter written from Lyme to her sister Cassandra. Jane mentions a Miss Armstrong with whom she walked on the Cobb and who 'seems to like people rather too easily; she thought the Downes pleasant'.

Lyme had also been on the Rev John Swete's itinerary during his travels ten years earlier in 1794. From Axminster, he had approached Lyme on horseback, entering the town on the Uplyme Road:

> "On entering the town, the descent became more rapid, falling through a very decent wide street to the sea, and at the bottom, very near the shore, we came to our inn, the Three Cups.

7. *Lyme Regis in about 1840 showing the old Three Cups Inn on the left. A coach stands outside the Custom House.*

Whilst our dinner was preparing, we walked from the Rooms to the fortifications, which seemed to possess strength enough to defend the town from the plunder of privateer. At this place was a pleasant walk, on a flat pavement, and a shed covered for the reception of company, over which several houses towered, and in an intermediate space waved the Tamarisk, its branches of a pale green, producing a most charming effect.

A narrow footway conducted up to the bathing machines, and further still to the pier, or Cobb as it is termed. At this spot the view of the Town and Cliffs beyond was uncommonly fine and romantic, the sloping ridge on which the house and church arose had a fine relief given it by the falling hill, and the Cliffs, behind which dipped diagonally and were, in seeing, strata of lead colour, marle or clay. The whole of this scenery was an intermixture of the

Picturesque and Romantic; overhung by the mountainous heights, the town was conspicuously beautiful.

Lyme however, from the cursory observations that I had been able to make, did not strike me as being an eligible place for Summer resort, for the country circumjacent is very hilly. It was void of trees, it had no picturesque scenery, no rides, no diversity of walks. The shore, when the tide had not far receded was pebbly, and neither well adapted for bathing, exercise or amusement. (Devon Record Office, 564M)

The years that John and Anna Rattenbury spent in Lyme appear to have been settled. Their first child, William, was christened there on 27 December 1801.

I remained at home about four years, being principally engaged in piloting and victualling ships. During this time, an American brig came into the bay, and I went off to her with three other men. As soon as we were on the deck, the prize-master ordered the people to bring up his pistols, and he detained me on board. He wanted me to pilot the brig into Weymouth because there was insufficient water to bring her into Lyme. I did as I was bid and he gave me twenty guineas in consideration of the service I had rendered.

On another occasion I was summoned to Bridport to take charge of a vessel. That same night a lieutenant, who belonged to the *Diamond* frigate, but who was in the *Greyhound* cutter, came on board to impress men. He took me and put me in confinement, with a man over the hatch to keep me down, while he overhauled other vessels lying there.

When he was gone, I said to the man guarding me: "Let me up and I'll give you a guinea". He accepted the offer and I got on deck and jumped overboard. But he gave the alarm, and the gang surrounded and re-captured me. They carried me back to the boat in triumph.

I had to find some way to escape so when daylight came I said to the lieutenant, "Let's go ashore and I'll show you where you can find some fine young fellows". He agreed and we went on shore. I pointed out a public-house, but finding none there he suspected me of a ruse to get free and ordered me back to the boat with the rest of his men. On the way, I saw my wife coming towards me. I entreated him to let me stop for a moment to speak to her, but this he gruffly refused, and in an angry tone ordered me instead toward the boat.

As soon as I got on board I was off again, through the water, and up the town. He followed with nine of this men, but my wife collared him. He threw her down and a scuffle ensued, in which the townspeople took part. Meanwhile I made my escape and got clear off.

Scenes like this, with a wife hindering the attempts of a gang to take her husband away, and with local people pitching in to help her, were repeated again and again along the south coast when a press was underway. Experienced sailors like Rattenbury were a priority with the press gangs because of their seafaring skills and experience, but those skills was of equal value to their families and friends, and to the local merchants who employed the men in the coasting and smuggling trades.

So unpopular were the press gangs in the south-west that parts of the coast were too dangerous for them to operate effectively. In his book *Hearts of Oak*, G J Marcus states that the Cornish Peninsula was off-limits to them, and that Portland in Dorset offered a man threatened with impressment 'unrivalled facilities for successful evasion'.

Rattenbury does not tell us when his encounter with the press gang took place. It could have been in the spring of 1803 because that is when the resumption of hostilities with France sent the gangs into action again. However, it is more likely to have been in late 1805 or early 1806 when Lieutenant Daniel Miller of His Majesty's Impress Service was extremely active against smugglers in east Devon. His gang's rendezvous point was Teignmouth although his regulating officer, Captain John Taylor Mitchell, was based at Exeter.

8. Greyhound *Excise cutter on a wind and chasing, 1794.*

The vessel which conveyed the press gang into Bridport was the *Greyhound*, a revenue cutter from Weymouth. The cutter's commander, Richard Wilkinson, would have assisted the gang in this way because, as a government officer, he was obliged to do so. It was also a way of reducing the risks of impressment for his own men.

As experienced seamen, revenue cutter crews were just the calibre of recruits needed by the navy therefore, despite being nominally exempt from the press, they sometimes got swept up, a fate which befell the twenty man crew of the Cowes cutter *Swan* in April 1807. The Cowes collector acted fast to get his men released and, in November 1807, seeking to avoid a repetition of the incident, he applied to the Customs Board for protection from impressment for the crews of his *Stork* and *Fox* cutters. This involved sending physical descriptions of fourteen men, most of them in their early twenties.

Despite the friction between the two services, customs officers did, as Rattenbury testifies, allow the Impress Service to use their cutters as Trojan horses, enabling the gang to enter a port secretly, before the seamen had a chance to flee.

The Impress Service had orders to impress any man caught smuggling, and working with the revenue service greatly improved their chances of doing so. As smugglers were most plentiful in the Beer area it was there, in 1806, that Miller and his gang concentrated their efforts. There were perks - if they caught a smuggler in possession of contraband then Miller, as the seizing officer, could claim from Customs an eighth share of the proceeds when the goods were condemned and sold at the Custom House.

The encounter between John Rattenbury and Daniel Miller at Bridport may have been their first, but it was not to be the last.

After this adventure, I went to reside at Beer and made a great many smuggling trips. Sometimes I was completely successful, but other times I had the mortification of witnessing the capture of my property because of the vigilance of officers who, like harpies, were continually hovering round the shore looking out for prey. The foremost of these was the lieutenant of the *Greyhound* from whose clutches I had so recently escaped.

From him I had a narrow escape. It happened while I was at Weymouth. Learning he was hoping to pounce on me, I took refuge in a public-house where I was well acquainted with the landlord. The lieutenant, having obtained intelligence of my hiding-place, paid us a visit at about 2 o'clock in the morning. He roused us from sleep by swearing that if the landlord did not come down and open the door, he would fire at him through the window, and force an entrance.

As soon as the alarm was given, I climbed up the chimney and there I remained while he was inspecting the premises, which took about an hour. When he had gone, and all was quiet, I came down.

How dismal I must have looked! I was covered all over with soot, and because the space in which I had been confined had been so narrow, I had not only had difficulty in breathing, but had bruised myself considerably. Nevertheless my exultation at having once more escaped from the clutches of this keen-eyed lieutenant and indefatigable picaroon [rogue] triumphed over my pain.

Miller was certainly a worthy opponent for Rattenbury. An officer in charge of a press gang would have had to be assertive and tenacious, and Miller was. He did not like anyone getting the better of him, not even his commanding officer....

In April 1806, hearing a report that smugglers were on the coast near Teignmouth, Miller took his gang-boat and encountered the *Providence*, a sloop belonging to Weymouth. The smugglers escaped in their rowing boat, but Miller captured the ship and its substantial cargo of 162 kegs of spirits. These he took to the Custom House at Topsham. They were condemned and sold and he put in his claim for a share of profits. However, his senior officer, Captain Mitchell, also claimed a share even though he had not been involved in the seizure. Lt Miller was much vexed and wrote to the collector at Exeter. He quoted chapter and verse from the revenue laws, and cited customs precedents, in an effort to exclude Mitchell from his windfall. And he succeeded. Mitchell withdrew and Miller got his money.

With two royal navy officers fighting over such substantial rewards, Rattenbury's description of the lieutenant, and of other seizing officers, as 'harpies' is no exaggeration - they stood to gain almost as much from smuggling as the smugglers did!

The pursuit of my enemies was incessant and I was followed by them from place to place, like a stag hunted by hounds, or a bird worried by the sportsman. It wearied me and I decided to get rid of them by going privateering again. I therefore shipped myself on board the *Unity* cutter, a privateer vessel then fitting out for Weymouth. It was commanded by Captain Head.

The 92-ton *Unity* already had a colourful history. In April 1803 she was captured with a cargo of contraband aboard, taken into Falmouth and condemned. She was sold to her new owner - Joseph Horsford of Weymouth, who had been part-owner of the *Alert* in which Rattenbury had gone privateering in 1800 - on the condition that she was properly registered, which was done in Weymouth on 11 December 1804. She was awarded a Letter of Marque three days later. The captain was Timothy Head, and Rattenbury was one of his crew of thirty.

About February 1805 we went to sea, and after touching at Alderney to take in our stock of spirits and other refreshments, we steered our course towards Madeira, Tenerife, etc, in the hope of falling in with prizes. For ten weeks we continued cruising in this direction but without success. We then put into St Michael's [Sao Miguel in the Azores] for water etc. While we were in the roads, the captain gave part of the crew - the second commander and fifteen men - leave to go on shore for a day's pleasure. We spent the day together in the utmost concord and conviviality and, at about 7 o'clock in the evening - the time appointed for our return - we put off from shore. We got alongside the cutter but, when our commanding officer jumped, he upset the boat and we were all thrown into the water.

It was dreadful to be threatened with a watery grave. It was dark and, in accidents like this, drowning men often lay hold of one another so, to avoid the danger, I swam away as fast as I could. When all was quiet, I swam alongside the vessel. In doing so I encountered a man much exhausted, but still clinging to an oar, by which he was endeavouring to support himself. I gave him all the assistance I could and succeeded in getting him on board. Some of my shipmates had the good fortune to do the same, but two were so completely spent with fatigue, and had taken in so much water, that it was two or three days before they were properly recovered.

We mustered the men, called the names and found, with regret, that two were missing. Having lost the boat, we could not search for them and we never saw the poor fellows again. They had left the ship in the morning, full of gaiety, had spent the day in festive amusement, and in the evening the sea was their winding-sheet.

The next morning, the Portuguese succeeded in getting our boat and brought her off to us; but she was so shattered that we had to have her repaired before we put to sea again.

We went on another cruise which lasted about eight weeks, but that wasn't successful either. We steered for the beautiful island of Madeira, where we found another privateer belonging to Guernsey. Its captain told us that, the day before, several of his men had been impressed by *Le Egyptien* frigate, which then lay in sight. This caused such a panic among our men that everyone except myself and four others, went ashore. However, the frigate did not remain long in the roads, and after its departure, having got our men and the articles we stood in need of, on board, we immediately set a course for England. On our voyage homeward we saw several men-of-war, but our vessel was such a swift sailer that none could get up with us.

According to an Admiralty register, the *Egyptian,* (567 tons), which was captained by Thomas Cannell and had a crew of fifty men, was awarded a Letter of Marque on 13 July 1804 and therefore, like the *Unity,* may have been operating as a privateer.

In August 1805 we arrived at Beer, where all those afraid of being impressed were put on shore. The voyage was so unsuccessful that I made up my mind never again to engage in privateering, a resolution which I have kept ever since, and of which I have never repented.

During John's absence, Anna had given birth to a second child, Frances Nichols - named after Anna's mother. She was baptised in Lyme on 3 June 1805 so either Anna had taken William and gone to live there during her husband's absence at sea, or she had not gone to Beer with Rattenbury when he fled the press gang. A more likely explanation is that most of his troubles with the gang post-dated his voyage to the Azores on the *Unity*, but without more evidence coming to light it is impossible to be sure. What is likely is that soon after Rattenbury's return in August 1805, the whole family went to live in Beer.

On my return home, I engaged ostensibly in the trade of fishing, but I was principally employed in that of smuggling, in which I had many varied and extraordinary adventures, the sort that usually attend such a precarious occupation. I have set them down in chronological order, and they, together with events to which they gave rise, will form the largest part of the ensuing narrative.

The Rattenburys of Beer 1777-1835

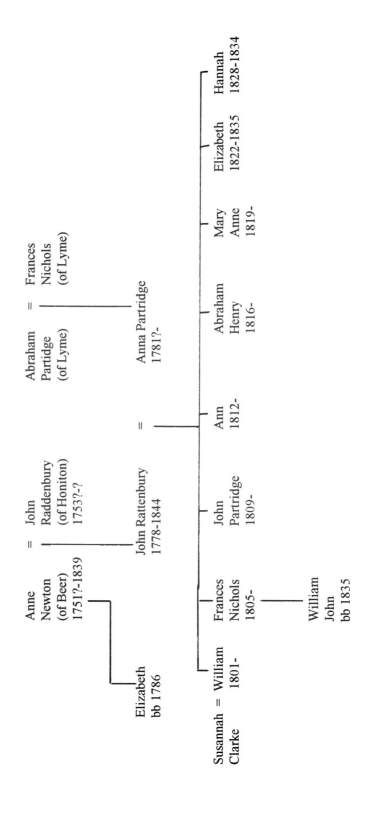

CHAPTER 7

Smuggling, Capture, and Escape
1806

It was in August 1805, when he was 26, that John Rattenbury's smuggling career began in earnest. He had found that more honest occupations were, as sources of income, either erratic (piloting), unreliable (privateering), or plain unexciting (fishing). With a family to support, smuggling offered him the best financial return on his skills. The activity was not without its risks. It brought him into conflict with Daniel Miller and his press gang, and with the local customs officers and revenue cutter captains whose duty it was to prevent smuggling and capture smugglers.

The preventive service was made up of officers who pursued their duties on land (the riding officers, known collectively as the landguard); those who pursued their duties at sea (revenue cutter commanders and their crews); and those who pursued their duties on land and sea (the preventive boatmen, known as the waterguard). In general, the revenue cutters patrolled at sea ready to board smuggling vessels returning from France or the Channel Islands with contraband; groups of boatmen, stationed at strategic points on the coast, either watched for landings from the shore or, using their oared boats, patrolled just offshore where the revenue cutters could not reach; and the riding officers looked out for, and tried to intercept, contraband being transported inland. In ports, additional officers were needed to search vessels at the quayside (land surveyors and landwaiters); and at busy beaches like Sidmouth, Seaton and Beer, there were officers who searched vessels anchored just offshore (coastwaiters). Duties overlapped - riding officers co-operated with boatmen on the shore, and boatmen or coastwaiters assisted riding officers inland.

How were these groups organised? Who were they answerable to? In each of the major ports there was a Custom House headed by a collector and a comptroller, who ran the customs affairs of the port and its district. It was to them that the riding officers, boatmen, landwaiters and coastwaiters in their area reported. Each of these outports had at least one, sometimes two, revenue cutters attached. There were Customs outports in all the major ports, including Southampton, Portsmouth, Cowes, Poole, Lyme, Weymouth, Exeter, Dartmouth and Falmouth. The collector and comptroller of each were answerable to the Customs Board in London, through which the

Government issued orders and conducted its customs and anti-smuggling policies.

In the 18th and early 19th Centuries, with import duties always on the increase, so was smuggling, and so too was the size of the preventive operation. Smuggling was subject to periodic declines but these were rarely the result of the effectiveness of the preventive service, or the acumen of the politicians. For example, the Peninsular War 1808-1814 had a dire effect on the trade because the French closed their ports to British merchants, even smugglers. With duties remaining high, the downturn lasted only as long as the circumstances prevailed.

Government policy ensured that smuggling was a thriving industry, and for some people it became a way of life. It not only supported smugglers and their families, but the families of the men who earned their livelihoods in the preventive service. It must have occurred to more than one boatman or revenue captain that the cessation of smuggling might also bring to an end the means whereby he too earned his living, so a fine balance had to be struck if the amount of contraband seized was to satisfy the local collector, and the Board in London, without putting the smugglers out of business.

Over the centuries, the methods used by the smugglers varied, and they were quick to adapt to changes in prevention. The 18th Century was a period when large smuggling vessels with large crews landed large cargos of contraband on open beaches, often in daytime, and when large gangs of men - like the Beer Gang - were used to protect the goods as they were transported inland towards their markets. The famous Isaac Gulliver of Dorset also belonged to this era. John Rattenbury belongs to a later era.

In the early 19th Century, when smugglers were up against a larger customs operation, they found it prudent to engage in smaller, more secretive ventures which depended on guile for success rather than on brute force. The transitional period was 1790-1810, the period of Rattenbury's earliest ventures.

During these two decades, the Beer and Seaton smugglers would either use their own vessels to fetch spirits from Guernsey or Alderney, or would rendezvous at sea with large cutters which had ferried the goods from the Channel Islands for them. Sometimes these cutters carried the spirit in large barrels, called pipes, and decanted it into smaller kegs when the local 'tub boats' came alongside to take it off. The crew of a tub boat would then either run the goods ashore immediately, or sink them a few miles offshore to be retrieved later when both the landguard and the waterguard were off their guard! The kegs would, of course, be water-proof and, when sunk roped together in rafts, would be weighted down with stones and marked by a small float. Those on board the tub boat would take bearings from the shore so that the contraband could be located later and fished up with grappling hooks. Fishing for tubs was called creeping. It was a fruitful pastime for smugglers, who knew exactly where to look, but a gruelling one for boatmen and revenue cutter crews who usually did not.

9. *Revenue boatmen creeping for tubs*

If a small smuggling vessel, returning from the Channel Islands with its cargo of tubs, was chased by a revenue cutter, and there was time available to sink the rafts in an orderly manner, this was done. But in an emergency, the kegs would be thrown overboard by the crew to lighten the load and dispose of the evidence. This action posed a problem for the captain of the pursuit vessel who then had to decide whether to stop and fish up the contraband (without which a conviction was unlikely) and risk losing the smugglers, or continue the pursuit of the smugglers and risk losing the contraband. Given that the contraband would, when sold, yield him a handsome profit, the decision for some revenue cutter captains was very easy to make!

After his privateering voyage on the *Unity*, Rattenbury's first two smuggling trips were not to the Channel Islands to fetch contraband but, surprisingly, east along the coast to Christchurch:

My first voyage, in an open boat, was to Christchurch, where we took in a cargo of contraband goods. On our return, we safely landed all of it. We were so elated with our success that we went straight back to the same port. However, on our way, we fell in with the *Roebuck* tender. A warm chase ensured and, in firing at us, a man by the name of Slaughter, who was on board the tender, had the misfortune to blow his arm off. The enemy managed to come up with us and we were captured. When we were taken on board, the captain was in such a rage about the accident that he swore he would put us all on board a man-of-war. Soon after he hailed a boat belonging to the government service, calling for it to come alongside so that he could carry out his threat, but she passed on without paying any attention.

To get the wounded man ashore, the captain got out his own boat. While this was going on, an opportunity presented itself and, unnoticed by anyone, I stowed myself away in her. There was so much confusion that my presence was not perceived and when the boat reached the shore I left it and got clear off.

That same night, I borrowed a boat and went alongside the tender to rescue all my companions, and three kegs of gin! We landed at Weymouth, from where we made our way home. I was proud of my victory, and considered it a great achievement.

In the late 18th Century, Christchurch was as well known for its smuggling as Beer. Such was the pitch of its illegal activity that in 1784, on the beach at Mudeford, a battle took place between the crews of two revenue service cutters and a royal navy ship, and a gang of smugglers. Twenty years later Rattenbury was transporting goods from Christchurch to Beer, so what sort of arrangement then existed that required contraband to be smuggled *along* the coast from one notorious smuggling area to another?

We don't know but about this time, two vessels with Beer and Seaton connections - the *Mayflower* owned by John Violett of Seaton and John Robilliard of Alderney; and *Brothers* owned by Daniel French, Thomas Wills and Thomas Bidney - were seized for smuggling and taken into Southampton and Portsmouth respectively. Were Devon smugglers co-operating with those in Dorset and Hampshire

Rattenbury says he went to Christchurch in an open boat. It was probably like the *Fly* of Beer, a lugsail boat seized on 7 August 1805 by the mate of the *Sea Gull*, a Poole revenue cutter commanded by John Carter, and based at Brownsea Island. *Fly* was hauled up onto Chesil Beach. Already badly damaged, it was broken up.

The next smuggling trips Rattenbury made *were* to Alderney and they took place in the winter of 1805/1806 when Sir John Doyle, commander in chief of HM Forces in Guernsey and Alderney offered a reward of fifty guineas to anyone with information leading to the capture of the person, or persons, who on the night of 22 February 1806 bored holes in the bottom of one the boats belonging to HM Revenue!

> The same winter, I made seven voyages in a smuggling vessel which had just been built. Five were successful and two were failures; then she was laid up.
>
> In the spring of 1806 I went to Alderney where we took in a cargo. Returning, we fell in with the *Duke of York* cutter. There was a fog so we got close to her boat without realising she was there. Unable to make our escape, we were put on board and the crew picked up some of our

kegs, which were floating nearby. We had sunk the principal part previously so, when we were secured, the captain called us into his cabin and said that if we would take up the kegs for him, he would give us our boat and liberty. He gave his honour as a gentleman so we readily agreed, pointed out where they lay, and took them up for him. He was not as good as his word. Instead he disgracefully departed from it and a fresh breeze springing up to the eastward, he steered away hard for Dartmouth.

10. Dartmouth Castle today

Coming alongside the castle at Dartmouth, while the cutter was going at six knots, I jumped overboard. The cutter had a boat in her stern and this they immediately lowered down with a man. To him the captain exclaimed: "If you do not bring him back, you shall go in his stead".

I succeeded in getting on shore, and concealed myself among some bushes. Two women saw me go into the thicket and inadvertently told the boat's crew, so I was immediately retaken. Exhausted with fatigue and loss of blood - having cut myself in several different places - I was carried on board. I was in such a state that my own shipmates could not help laughing at me. The captain, however, was aggravated:

"I'll put you on board a man-of-war, and send you to the East Indies!" he cried.

"You old rascal!" I replied, which sharpened his anger still more.

61

As soon as the cutter was brought to an anchor, the captain went on shore. About an hour afterwards, a lieutenant and his gang from Dartmouth came on board.

"What a fine set of young lads you have here!" the lieutenant said to the mate, and expressed a wish to take us on shore with him, but the mate would not consent during the absence, and without the orders, of the captain.

The following morning the captain came back on board and, with an escort of the cutter's people, and of constables, took us to the town hall in Dartmouth to be tried by the magistrates. We were each sentenced to pay a fine of £100, or go on board a man-of-war, or to gaol, whichever we pleased.

After a brief consultation, we agreed unanimously to go to gaol, upon which we were all crammed into a most deplorable hole, one in which they were accustomed to confine vagrants. It seemed to have been constructed along the lines of the Black Hole of Calcutta therefore, at 6 o'clock, being heartily sick of the place, I told my companions that they might do as they pleased but I was going to go on board a man-of-war. Hearing this, they said they would too and, having communicated our wish, we were liberated from our doleful confinement, and entered for the *Kite* brig, then lying in the Downs.

The same night, we were removed to the *Safeguard* brig, which then lay in Dartmouth roads. At the time, the captain was absent, but when he came on board the next morning, he called us up and asked questions about our case. When we told him that the captain of the cutter had promised us four gallons of gin, he immediately went on board the cutter himself to get them. He gave them to the steward, and told him to let us have two bottles at a time.

We received the first two, and after drinking them, we all began to be pretty merry. It was then I went on the quarter-deck and asked the captain if he would allow me to go on board the cutter, because I had some private communications to make to the captain. He readily consented, little imagining that I was forming a scheme to regain my liberty. A boat was lowered down, and the master of the ship, and four men, went with me to the cutter.

Once on board, I was asked to take something to drink, which I did, noticing that the master and some officers, busily engaged in conversation on the quarter-deck, were doing likewise. I also noticed that the main-sail had been partly hoisted and therefore neither the master, nor the boat's crew, could command a prospect of the shore. I went forward, looked around and, seeing that the coast was clear, immediately jumped down on the bobstay.

Approaching was a little boat with a fisherman in it. With my finger I signalled to him to come and drop under the bows. This he swiftly did, and in less than five minutes he landed me at Kingswear, opposite Dartmouth. I gave him a pound note for the assistance he had rendered and then made my way to Brixham, five miles away. I walked, or rather ran, the first mile, then borrowed a horse from a farmer and rode the remaining four. In Brixham I hired a fishing smack and in that got safely home.

I later learned that I was probably in Brixham by the time my escape was detected, and that several marines and sailors were dispatched in different ways to search for me. Also, that as a result of my escape, the officers kept a very sharp look-out upon my companions, who had been left behind.

This particular episode highlights the relationship between smugglers and the public at large. When Rattenbury escaped it was in the knowledge that local people would be more likely to help than hinder him. He always had about his person sufficient money for bribes, money which the cutter's crew appear not to have found or, perhaps, never even to have searched for?

What is equally interesting is the relationship between the cutter captain and the smugglers, and the confidence with which Rattenbury and his associates genuinely expected to exchange their sunken contraband for their freedom. Such deals cannot have been unusual.

The *Duke of York* does not appear to have been based at Dartmouth, where the local revenue cutter was the *Industry* captained by James Needs. At about this time, off Berry Head, Needs seized a large open boat with 135 casks, and a sloop carrying 94 casks.

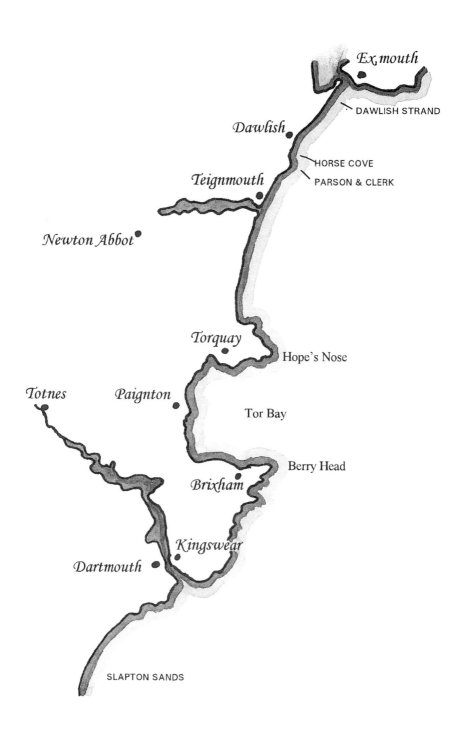

Ex mouth

DAWLISH STRAND

Dawlish

HORSE COVE

PARSON & CLERK

Teignmouth

Newton Abbot

Torquay

Hope's Nose

Totnes

Paignton

Tor Bay

Berry Head

Brixham

Kingswear

Dartmouth

SLAPTON SANDS

DARTMOUTH to EXMOUTH

CHAPTER 8

Cornish Adventures
1806-1807

After his narrow escape, and despite the very real dangers of prison and impressment, Rattenbury continued to smuggle, and found it sufficiently rewarding to be able to invest the profits in a variety of smuggling vessels, usually in partnership with others. The first, in 1806, was a galley.

At the beginning of the 19th Century, smugglers started using large oared boats to transport contraband across the Channel. The idea may have come from 'guinea boats' first used in about 1798 when the currency of France collapsed. Smugglers were quick to exploit the French need for gold sovereigns by smuggling them from England. For this they used galleys 45ft to 50ft in length and manned by up to 36 oarsmen. In some weeks, up to £10,000 worth of gold was smuggled into France. The galleys were made in Calais because in England the building of boats longer than 28ft was banned. They were fast and, not being dependent on the wind, more manoeuvrable than the revenue cutters, which they successfully evaded. Very few guinea boats were seized. News of their success must have spread quickly among the smuggling fraternity, who started employing similar boats.

> Soon after my return home, I purchased part of a galley, in which I made several successful voyages. On one occasion, I very narrowly escaped being taken. Returning one night from Alderney, we fell in with a custom house boat, by which we were chased. The crew fired at us. When they came up, we told them we belonged to the *Alarm* lugger. Darkness befriended us, the stratagem succeeded, and we got off. We later had the misfortune to lose the galley at sea.

The *Alarm* mentioned by Rattenbury was a revenue lugger based at Exeter and commanded by Captain John Eales. All large sailing vessels had oared boats which they used to transfer goods and men from ship to shore, and back again and, in the case of revenue vessels, for patrolling and creeping.

> In June, with two other men, I went in an open boat to Alderney to get kegs. On our voyage home, about mid-channel, we were chased and captured by the *Humber* sloop, commanded by Captain Hill. He took myself and my companions, the boat, and all, into Falmouth, to which port the sloop belonged.

11. A Revenue cutter and its boat

As soon as we arrived we asked to be sent on shore to be tried, but the captain refused. Instead he took us to sea again, on a cruise, therefore it was not until 20 July that we were brought before the magistrates in Falmouth. Having heard the case, they committed us to prison.

The trial finished late in the afternoon so the captain took us on board his ship for the night. In the morning, we came on shore and were put into two post-chaises to be taken to Bodmin gaol. There were two constables to take care of us and, as our guards stopped at almost every public-house we came to, towards evening they were pretty merry. I decided to take advantage of this and looked for a way to escape.

We arrived at the *Indian Queen*, a public-house a few miles from Bodmin, and while the constables were taking their potations, I bribed the drivers not to interfere.

The constables, having finished their drinks, ordered us back into the chaise. We refused. A scuffle ensued and one of them collared me. Some blows were exchanged in encountering the other constable, who called upon the drivers to aid and assist, but they said it was their duty to attend to the horses. We soon got the upper-hand of our opponents and, seeing a cottage near, I ran towards it. A woman was there and she kindly showed me through her house and into the garden. She pointed out the road.

I had gone about a mile when, looking back, I saw someone following me so I concealed myself in a ditch. When the person came up, he hailed me by name. It was my fellow-prisoner. He too had made his escape through the aid of the woman at the cottage. We went on together.

Towards evening we met a party of men, smugglers like ourselves. We told them about our adventures and they behaved very handsomely towards us, taking us that night to a place called Newquay, where we slept.

The next morning we got up very early and, from a landlord, hired three horses to take us to Mevagissey. He came with us to take them back. At Mevagissey we had the good fortune to meet a friend. Our money was almost exhausted so he lent us £10 and we hired a boat. It took us to Budleigh Salterton which, as the wind was easterly, was the most convenient place to land.

On the following day we walked on and in the evening, to our great joy, arrived safe at Beer.

Here is more evidence of fraternity between smuggling communities. It was in Mevagissey in 1792 that the *Lively*, the Alderney smuggling cutter of Robilliard, le Cocq and Sandford, had been built.

The *Indian Queen* no longer exists but a town called Indian Queens, named after it, has grown up around the site.

At the end of July, I went again in an open boat to Alderney. We took in a cargo of contraband articles, with which we arrived safe home. At about the same time, I met an old captain with whom I had been acquainted for several years. He was about to leave his vessel for another, so he recommended me to the owners who appointed me to succeed him. This vessel was called the *Trafalgar*.

The *Trafalgar* was registered at Exeter on 17 February 1806 as being owned by mariner Robert Smith and yeoman Thomas Bastin, both of East Budleigh. Robert Smith was her first master, William Farrant her second. Rattenbury took over from Farrant on 4 October 1806.

My first voyage in her was to Newport for coals, and we completed it in seven days. We then went to Leith for a cargo of culm, accomplishing that in eighteen days. I then received orders to get a standing bowsprit and steer for the islands [Channel Islands] for the purpose of smuggling.

The length of a vessel's bowsprit determined how fast it could travel. Only naval and revenue vessels were allowed to have bowsprits longer than two-thirds the length of the hull. Local customs officials could refuse to register a vessel if it had an illegal bowsprit, but that did not stop owners altering them after registration. If Rattenbury received orders to go smuggling in the *Trafalgar* then who else could have issued them but Smith and Bastin, the owners?

Rattenbury took over on the *Trafalgar* in 1806, the same year Lt Daniel Miller and his press gang were very active in the Beer area, as is evident in a letter Miller wrote to the Board on 8 November 1806 from his base at Teignmouth:

> "Since I have been employed in the Impress Service at this Port, I have made every possible exertion to suppress smuggling on this coast, which has been carried on to a great extent about Beer and Seaton; and I have been fortunate enough within these six or seven months to seize the following goods and vessels. As I have been to great expense fitting out boats for the sole purpose of intercepting the smugglers on this coast, I trust, Gentlemen, that you will allow me a moiety on the Providence and Speedwell's cargos."

There followed a list of his seizures:

> "March 21 - Seized floating on the water, hove over board from several Beer boats, 19 4-gallon kegs of spirits.
> April 4 - Seized the sloop Providence with 162 4-gallon kegs of spirits.
> July 4 - Seized floating on the water, 12 4-gallon kegs of spirits.
> October 29 - Seized floating on the water, 50 4-gallon kegs of spirits.
> November 5 - Seized the Speedwell, lugsail boat of Beer with 24 4-gallon kegs of spirits, all of which is returned to His Majesty's Custom House, Exeter." (PRO. Exeter Letterbooks CUST 64/16)

Two months later, in January 1807, John Rattenbury again encountered the formidable Lt Miller:

I made five successful voyages to Alderney, but on the last, when we were returning and had nearly arrived at our destination, we fell in with a gang-boat commanded by Lt Miller. The weather was so hazy it happened before I was aware of it. As soon as I saw the danger, I ordered a man to the mast-head to loose the gaff-topsail. Having a fine breeze we bore away, but she came up again. When she was almost alongside, I headed into the wind. They did the same, but during the chase their mast went overboard allowing us to get clear off. We sunk our goods and steered again for Alderney.

When I landed I sent a pilot to take charge of the vessel, giving instructions to sail round about the island while I got ready the goods we were going to put on board. We were not able to load the vessel as quickly as I hoped because the revenue officers were keeping a very sharp look-out, so the crew took her out to sea again leaving me ashore. Later, they tried to put in at the pier, but could not do so without letting the anchor go, and in spite of the directions I gave them, they ran the vessel onto the rocks.

I immediately got a boat and pushed off. I reached them, but the vessel was in a deplorable state, with the sea breaking over her, and her bottom striking with tremendous force against the shingles. I knew she could not hold together much longer so I ran below and snatched up my pocket-book. I jumped into the boat with my companions. We got clear only just in time for the vessel rent asunder and separated into two parts, her lower works from her upper.

As soon as I reached the shore I mustered all the hands I could, and by our indefatigable exertions, we succeeded in recovering most of the materials from the wreck.

Four days after this disaster, I put the goods and the men on board another vessel, and sent them home, but during the night they fell in with the *Liberty* brig and *Pluto* sloop-of-war which took them prisoners and captured the cargo. The same day, having settled my business in the island, I went on board a vessel I had hired. It was laden with contraband goods and we were chased by those same king's ships, but by management in sailing, got off and made a good voyage.

The vessel which Rattenbury put his men aboard was the *Mary* of Sidmouth, which was captured by the HMS Brig *Liberty*, commanded by Lt John Codd, on 30 January 1807. There was a chase first, during which the *Mary*'s cargo of 180 kegs was thrown overboard, only to be fished up by the *Liberty*'s crew. Lt Codd wrote to the Board on 1 February informing them that he had:

> "*captured on the 30 January, the* Mary *of Sidmouth, a smuggling vessel, [and] her cargo of spirits. Manned with seven men, they were asked on coming on board if they would volunteer for His Majesty's Service. They refused, but [were] impressed, six... on board HM sloop* Pluto, *and one on board the brig under my command. And understanding by a late Act of Parliament that there is £50 a head for all men taken in smuggling vessels, I request your Honble Board will grant me an order to receive the same.*" (PRO. Dartmouth Letterbooks CUST 65/10)

Some of six men impressed aboard the *Pluto* - John Evans, Robert Barratt, James Webber, John Robins, and William and John Weekes - were Rattenbury's crew from the *Trafalgar*. They were still on the ship four months later when the *Pluto*'s captain, Richard Janverin, confirmed their presence to the Customs Board.

In October 1807 Lt Codd faced the same problem as Daniel Miller when he learned that Lt Bird of the *Ant* schooner, which had been sailing with the *Liberty* at the time of the capture, was claiming a share of the *Mary*'s cargo. Lt Codd was indignant and wrote to the Board:

> *"I beg leave to acquaint you that he [Lt Bird] neither aided nor assisted in capturing the said vessel, but on the contrary, shortened sail instead of aiding in the chase, and I totally object in his sharing."* (PRO. Dartmouth Letterbooks CUST 65/10)

This disagreement arose because, under naval rules of engagement pertaining to prizes, Lt Bird had a claim, whereas under customs regulations, he did not. Not surprisingly each lieutenant chose to argue in favour of whichever rule benefited him the most.

It wasn't only officers in the navy and the Impress Service who argued over the rewards for captured contraband. In February 1807, 33 casks of spirit were found floating near the shore at Alderney and seized by the boat belonging to the local revenue cutter, the *Lion* commanded by Captain Blake; but the Governor of Guernsey, insisting they were wreck goods, claimed them for himself.

Undeterred by the fate of the crew captured by Lt Codd, Rattenbury was soon smuggling again:

> A few months later I went with three other men in an open boat to the islands [Channel Islands]. We made two good voyages. We then bought an eight-oared boat which had belonged to the *Alarm* cutter, but had been condemned at the custom house. In this we succeeded very well.

It was on 28 July 1806 that Captain Eales of the *Alarm* lugger reported that his oared boat was useless and returned it to the store at the Custom House in Topsham. It is not known how soon afterwards Rattenbury and his unnamed associates bought it.

> In the fall of the same year, we went to St Helen's [Isle of Wight] and bought a small vessel called the *Lively*. Crossing the channel was a disaster because we were chased by a French privateer, and the man at the helm was shot. The privateer came up with us, but the captain was so affected by what had taken place that he generously gave up the vessel.
>
> We afterwards made three voyages in her, but she was so leaky they were accomplished only at the extreme hazard of our lives. We were afraid to venture out in her again in that state, so we had her hauled onto the beach, and she was stripped to undergo repairs.

We then bought a vessel called the *Neptune*, in which we made three prosperous voyages. On the fourth she was wrecked while going into Alderney. It happened in one of the most violent gales of wind from the north I ever remember. On this melancholy occasion, 23 vessels broke from their moorings. Only three held on and rode out the gale: a custom house cutter, a merchant brig, and a fishing smack. It was a shocking and tremendous spectacle to see so many vessels drifting about, their crews at their wits' end. Not one person was able to help another, and none dared venture from land to give assistance.

Our vessel was driven on shore and went to pieces. I and my companions escaped a watery grave only by jumping from vessel to vessel till we got into one in which we could wait for the tide to go back, and for the violence of the tempest to subside. It was the Brixham vessel that came off best.

A fishing smack from that same port went into Alderney in the midst of the gale, and it was with its captain that I made an agreement to take myself and my goods to the mainland. This he did and I got home with all my cargo after all, without meeting any further disaster.

Misfortunes, it is said, seldom come alone. This is so true, as we found out, for the vessel we had hauled up on the beach [ie the *Lively*], had been repaired and was therefore at sea in this violent gale. It put into Brixham where the officers [customs officers], suspecting what she was, went on board and seized her. I, being bondsman for her in the sum of £160 was arrested a few months afterwards. Unable to obtain the smallest mitigation, I was obliged to pay the sum, which was a great shock to my circumstances.

The only vessel by the name of *Lively* which Rattenbury is recorded as being the owner - in partnership with another Beer mariner called William Westlake - was registered at Exeter on 28 December 1807.

It is stated in the Exeter records that, on 21 May 1807, the sole owners of a vessel called *Neptune* were Exeter men, John Shute and Abraham Tozer, and George Shute of Crediton. Was this the same *Neptune* as the one wrecked at Alderney?

One of the difficulties in trying to track down in the records which vessel was which is the commonality of some the names given to them. How inconsiderate these ship-builders and ship-owners were, giving nary a thought for us poor researchers who, nearly two centuries later, would be straining their eyes over the shipping registers!

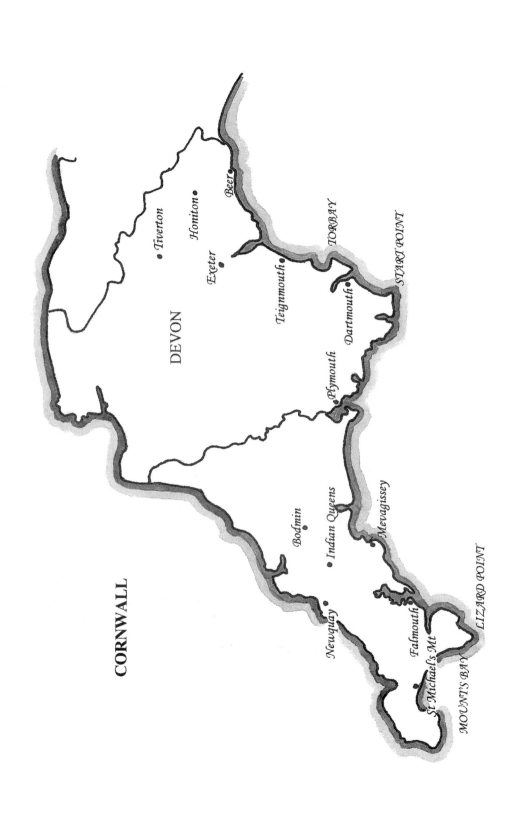

CHAPTER 9

Smuggling around Beer and Seaton
1807

When a run was successful, John Rattenbury would land his contraband on the Devon coast, often in the vicinity of Beer; but where exactly? Where did the other local smuggling organisations land their contraband? And who else, apart from Daniel Miller and the men in his press gang, did they have to contend with in doing so?

In 1807, the coast from Axmouth in the east to Teignmouth in the west was under the jurisdiction of the Custom House in Exeter.

12. Exeter Custom House

Robert Head was the riding officer for Seaton and Beer, William Webber the riding officer at Branscombe, and Charles Wild, both riding officer and coastwaiter at Sidmouth. A preventive boat and its crew was stationed at Beer but, inconveniently for the preventive effort, they were controlled by the port of Lyme. On 14 March 1807, the collector at Exeter, J P Wright, pointed out to the Board that:

"The crew of the Boat at Beer, being paid at the Port of Lyme, and under the superintendence of the officers of that Port, we have no knowledge of any threats or obstructions they may have met with from the smugglers, whereby they may have been prevented from performing their duty." (PRO. Exeter Letterbooks CUST 64/16)

The chief officer of the Beer boat, or sitter as the post was then designated, was Thomas Head, the riding officer's son. It was not unusual for a local surname to be shared between smugglers and revenue men, as appears to have been the case with the Heads of Seaton and Beer.

Despite their different paymasters, the boatmen of Beer co-operated with the other customs officers. For example, in April 1806, riding officer Robert Head spotted smuggling boats off Beer Head and sent his son Thomas and William Lyons, the Beer boat's extraman, to a field called White Cliff to keep watch in case someone ashore tried to light fires to try to warn the vessels off. The boatmen saw two men start fires with straw and tinder. One was James Orley the younger, a Beer fisherman, who was arrested. The boatmen also noted that other fires had been lit about half a mile away in the other direction.

It is obvious from Rattenbury's account that 1806 was a busy year for smugglers, and Robert Head confirms this. On 2 January 1807 he informed the collector at Exeter that in the Beer and Seaton area smuggling was not only worse than it had been the previous winter, but as bad as he could remember. The Beer and Seaton smugglers who owned their own vessels and were continually working in the smuggling trade on their own account had, in November and December 1806, twice gone out to a large cutter anchored just off Beer to take off her cargo but Robert Head was unable to discover where they were bringing the kegs ashore:

"which is convincing proof to me that the goods must be landed at or about Beer and Seaton when they can do it quietly among their own Friends and Relations." (PRO. Exeter letterbooks CUST 64/16)

After the cutter's second visit, Head watched impotently as ten Beer and Seaton boats, and two from Budleigh Salterton, took up the sunken rafts of kegs which had been taken out of her. The cutter was identified as the *Lively* of Alderney, which had also made trips to the Dorset and Hampshire coasts. She was seized off Portland with eighteen pipes of spirits and a quantity of empty casks, and taken into Portsmouth.

Lively was a common name for vessels and Rattenbury was associated with one, or possibly two, of that name. However the one mentioned by Robert Head was surely the cutter owned by Peter le Cocq, Thomas Robilliard, and John and William Sandford of Alderney, which was broken up in Bridport in 1809. If Thomas Robilliard was the same Robilliard who then lived on the quayside at Weymouth, then the loss of the *Lively* must have contributed to him going out of business in 1810.

If any more evidence were needed of the connection between the smugglers of Beer and Alderney in 1806 and 1807, then it can be supplied by Beer boatman Jacob Good, who detained a small boat belonging to John Sandford because its dimensions were not legal for the purpose for which it had been built, ie. fishing around Alderney. Customs officers on Guernsey also suspected some Alderney merchants of using John Tany, a suspected smuggler and master of the *Rover*, as an agent.

The *Lively* was not the only cutter involved in the trade. There were many incidents of large smuggling cutters - up to 100 tons according to Captain Eales of the *Alarm* lugger - seen on the coast of Devon between January and March 1807. Captain Durell, commander of the sea fencibles spotted one; William Webber at Branscombe, and Charles Wild of Sidmouth saw others. So concerned was the Board at the increase in smuggling, that they asked the Exeter collector to conduct a survey of the coast. The final report is quoted here in full because of the excellent description it gives of the east Devon coast as Rattenbury and his fellow smugglers knew it. It pinpoints the places cargos were landed, suggests how the contraband was carried off the beach, and records which routes were probably used to transport it inland.

> *"From **Axmouth Haven** - the Eastern limit of the Port - to **Seaton**, the beach is open and accessible at all parts for about a mile in length. The mode of communication with the interior is easy, by means of several bye-roads which branch off different ways from the village of Seaton. There is also an opportunity of conveying contraband goods in boats further on, four miles up the River Axe to Colyford Bridge, for which reason we are of [the] opinion that a Riding Officer might now be placed to great advantage at Seaton in the room of [ie in place of] William Raddon, deceased (late Riding Officer from Axmouth Haven to Branscombe Mouth), to communicate with the Riding Officers of this Port stationed at Beer and Branscombe, [and] with the officer of the Port of Lyme stationed at Axmouth. Small parties of soldiers stationed at Seaton, at Colyton about three miles to the north of*

Seaton, and at Beer, within constant call of those officers, would tend materially to check the progress of smuggling, it being impossible for any officer single-handed to attempt to detain the persons whom he may find conveying smuggled goods, especially where they go in gangs and armed.

From Seaton the beach begins to assume a bold aspect and there is no landing place for about a quarter of a mile, [where] at a place called **Seaton Chan**, a small break in the cliff communicates immediately with the road leading from Seaton to Beer. This place is not much frequented.

The cliff continues about a quarter of a mile to **Seaton Hole** [about midway between Seaton and Beer], a convenient landing place, seeming much frequented, close to the road above mentioned, with another bye-lane leading up through the fields.

The cliff continues from hence very strong about half a mile to **Beer Beach**, which is open for about a hundred yards but, we understand, not much used as a landing place, being close under the house of Mr Robert Head, Riding Officer, who has it, of course, continually under his eye.

From this place the strong cliff continues to **Pounsfold [Pound's Pool]**, about a quarter of a mile below Beer. The goods

13. Beer beach. Looking towards Beer Head and Pound's Pool, 1829

are landed under the cliff and drawn up by ropes to the top, about fifty feet. This place is contiguous to several small lanes.

From hence the strong cliff continues about a mile to **Hooken.** *At this place, some years since, about ten acres of the cliff separated from the mainland and fell into the sea, by which a small cove is formed to the eastward where great quantities of goods are landed, and carried up by a winding path, above half a mile in length, to the top, where a large furze brake affords shelter for the goods till they can be carried away.*

The cliff continues very strong for half a mile to **Mitchell's Stile.** *Goods are landed here at low water, and brought up a very narrow winding path, at least half a mile. Difficult of access, a temporary obstruction might be made here by means of a stop gate, or strong wall, placed on the top of the cliff, but it is impossible it could remain without constant attendance upon it.*

The cliff continues equally strong half a mile to **Branscombe Mouth,** *an opening in the cliff and a road leading up to Branscombe village, with a branch off leading to the Lyme Road. From this place the beach is open about half a mile by the receding of the cliff, which is however inaccessible [as far as]* **Withybush,** *another landing place, similar to Mitchell's Stile. Goods may be landed upon any part of the beach between these two last places, but cannot be carried up the cliff at any intervening point.*

The beach and cliff continue pretty much the same about a mile to **Littlecumbe Shut [Littlecombe Shoot],** *a good landing place, and a road leading up to the head of Branscombe village. The fences, in general, [are] very indifferent, so that the smugglers may cross them in any direction that best suits their purpose to avoid the Officers.*

The beach and cliff continue the same half a mile to **Weston Mouth,** *a good landing place with two roads leading from it on each side of the valley to the top of the hill, where are a variety of roads leading to the Lyme Road, to Sidbury, Sidford, etc. There are also many small footpaths into the woods and coppices, with which the sides of the valley are clothed.*

The cliff continues half a mile to **Little Weston,** *a recent place, very difficult of access, the goods being brought up a very high cliff with steps almost perpendicular.*

The cliff continues half a mile to **Salcombe Mouth,** *a good landing with a horse road from the landing up to Salcombe Village and thence communicating with the interior as to Weston Mouth.*

The cliff continues inaccessible to **Sidmouth,** *where is an open beach nearly a mile in length. The station of Mr Wild, Officer, [it is] consequently not much frequented by the smugglers. From hence strong, inaccessible cliffs continue about a mile to* **Laderham [Ladram] Bay,** *a good landing place adjoining the road from*

Sidmouth to Otterton, with bye-roads leading off in a number of directions to Newton Poppleford, Harpford, Ottery St Mary, etc.

The cliffs continue about two miles to **Otterton Haven,** *where considerable quantities of goods are landed both sides of the mouth of the River Otter. There are three intermediate places between Laderham [Ladram] Bay and Otterton Haven where goods are occasionally hauled up the cliff at least 200ft high, viz* **Chiselbury, Crean Point** *(or* **Brandy Head***), and* **Otterton Point***, about half a mile distant from each other.*

We are of the opinion that a Riding Officer, stationed at Otterton, with a small party of soldiers there, would conduce materially to check the progress of smuggling. This officer could communicate very easily with the Riding Officer at Sidmouth, three miles distant, and the Chief Boatman at Budleigh Salterton, four miles distant, and form a chain of intelligence which must ultimately thwart the scheme of the smugglers, it being notorious at present. The moment Mr Wild, the Riding Officer at Sidmouth, shows himself to the eastward of that place, signals by fires etc are immediately made, and the boats bear away to the Westward and land at Laderham, Weston, etc, before it is possible [for him to] arrive by land.

14. Caves at Ladram Bay 1842

The strong, bold cliff continues to a ledge of rocks running about a quarter of a mile into the sea, called **Otterton Ledge**, near Salterton Lime Kilns, adjoining to and forming the mouth of the River Otter (or Otterton Haven), where small vessels under 40 tons burthen, not sharp built, can lay in safety having from five to ten feet of water at Spring or high tides, when the smugglers can land their cargos on either side of the River, there being roads and lanes leading to Otterton, Sidmouth, Exeter, etc. From thence is an open beach half a mile in length.

Budleigh Salterton, again interrupted by the high cliff, continues half a mile to **Sherbrooke Lake** (or **Chan of Nouson**), between Budleigh Salterton and West Down Beacon, under which lies **The Floor**, much resorted to in winter, with a beach half a mile in length - an excellent landing place where the horses go close to the beach and immediately branch off, over West Down to Woodbury Hill (or Down), where are roads and lanes leading in all directions into the interior.

From hence the cliffs continue half a mile to **Littleham Cove**, a place much frequented, and where goods are landed and conveyed into the interior with great facility. A Riding Officer stationed at Littleham to confer with the Riding Officer at Lympstone, about four miles distance, and with the Tide Surveyor at Exmouth, about two miles, would prove of great utility in strengthening the guard along the coast. We are also of [the] opinion that a small party of soldiers might be placed to advantage at Exmouth

From Littleham the high cliff and beach continues to **Straight** [or **Strait**] **Point**, and thence to **Water Shut**, places much frequented formerly, but not of late years, where goods were landed on the beach and carried up the cliff by means of ladders, and from thence carried through Littleham to Withycombe, Exmouth, etc, having high cliffs, and open beach to the **Beacon** at **Exmouth**.

From hence the beach is quite open for about a mile, and called the Warren, the first landing place after which is at **Langstone Rock**, where there are a variety of small bye-lanes communicating with the roads leading to Starcross, Kenton, etc, and thence to Exeter, and also leading up to a large open tract of country called Haldon, over which a variety of roads lead into all parts of the interior.

From this place a strong cliff continues about a mile to **Winterton Steps**, a good landing place close to the road leading from Exeter to Dawlish, with several bye-paths across the adjoining furze brakes, and roads that lead to Haldon, as above.

The cliff continue from hence about half a mile to **Dawlish Strand**, which is quite open and accessible for more than half a *mile. The communication from Dawlish to the adjacent country is easy by means of a variety of roads, and there not being any Officer of this Revenue stationed here, we conceive that a Boat might be placed here to great advantage, or a Riding Officer, to communicate with the Officers at Starcross and Teignmouth. A small party of soldiers would also be highly useful at this place, being within the reach of the Officers, either at Teignmouth or Starcross, as occasion might require.*

*A very strong, high cliff continues about a mile below Dawlish to **Horse Cove**, a very strong sheltered landing place [where]; goods [are] carried up a steep cragged path to the top of the cliff into the road leading from Dawlish to Teignmouth.*

*The same sort of cliff continues about a mile to **Holcombe Cove**, or **Holcombe Hole**, sometimes called the **Parson & Clerk**, a break in the high cliff forming a small cove. Horses can come down to this place, but the roads - two leading up to Holcombe village - are very bad from the village. Several bye-roads branch off towards Haldon etc.*

*The strong cliff continues about a mile to **Teignmouth Den**, which is open about half a mile to the entrance of the River Teign, the Western boundary of the Port. Goods have been heretofore frequently landed on the Den, but since the Press Gang has been stationed at Teignmouth, it has been but little resorted to by the smugglers.*

The Officers and Men stationed at the different Signal Houses at Holcombe Down, West Downe Beacon, and Hooken Down, might prove very serviceable by conferring with and occasionally giving information to the Officers of this Revenue.

We beg leave to make one general remark, which will be applicable to all the places at which we have submitted the propriety of placing soldiers, viz. that the parties should be <u>*relieved*</u> *as* <u>*often*</u> *as the* <u>*convenience of the Service*</u> *will admit, in order to prevent their forming intimacies and connections with the smugglers, which might ultimately defeat the end for which they were stationed.*

On a full consideration of all the circumstances attending the Coast within the District of this Port, we are perfectly satisfied that it is utterly impracticable to give the smallest check to smuggling by means of Stop Gates, and that the most feasible mode of attaining that desirable object is to strengthen the Land Guard by a regular chain of Preventive Officers, assisted by parties of the Military, at all times within their reach." (PRO. Exeter Letterbooks CUST 64/16, 29 October 1807)

This then was the situation in 1807, when even the dragoons drafted in to assist customs officers could be expected to be tempted into collusion. Obstruction by members of the local community was commonplace, with revenue officers treated with scant respect by local merchants, if John Violett's example is anything to go by.

Violett was not a native of Seaton, but had lived there since at least 1783 when he married Ann Hatson. They had seven children, all born between 1783 and 1805. On 29 September 1805 Violett took out a lease on a plot of ground right on the beach at Seaton. It included a yard. He held it for four years, until June 1809 when he passed it on to Seaton coal merchant, William Culverwell. In June 1807, while it was still in Violett's possession, riding officers Robert Head and William Webber, accompanied by two extramen from the Beer boat, attempted to search the premises, but Violett ordered them out. Ugly scenes followed, witnessed by townspeople.

The stated cause of the disagreement between the merchant and the customs men was Norwegian timber - delivered to Violett by Thomas Maxwell, captain of his ship *Good Intent*, owned by Violett in partnership with John Ford of Branscombe - on which Violett had not paid duty. Given Violett's undoubted connection with known smuggling vessels, they might also have been looking for contraband. It is perhaps significant that, a few months later, a general warning was issued to customs officers on the coast of east Devon that a Swedish boat was in the vicinity, and was believed to be about to unload a shipment of contraband.

There is little doubt that Violett dealt in both licit and illicit goods therefore it is impossible to say whether the Madeira wine he advertised for sale in the *Exeter Flying Post* of 4 August 1808 had been imported legally or not:

> "Madeira Wine. Just imported. 45 pipes and thirty hogsheads of the very best Old London Particular. For the accommodation of private families, a single pipe or hogshead will be sold at a time. For samples and further particulars, apply at the counting house of Joshua Rowe, merchant, Torpoint; at the Navy office, Plymouth; and Mr John Violett, merchant, Seaton. NB The purchasers may have it duty free or in the bonded cellar, much under the London prices."

CHAPTER 10

Evading Revenue Officers,
Naval Service, and the Militia
1808-1809

Riding officers, revenue boatmen, and dragoons were the human obstacles facing Rattenbury and his fellow smugglers on land, but there were obstacles at sea as well. Every outport on the south coast had one or two revenue cutters attached to it and they diligently patrolled the English Channel, particularly around the Channel Islands where, of course, the greatest concentration of smugglers was to be found. As a smuggler, Rattenbury had had encounters with cutters based at Falmouth and Dartmouth. Now it was the turn of Cowes.

Not long after this disaster, I bought part of a twelve-oared boat, which had a 54ft keep and was 60ft aloft. We made a voyage to Alderney in her and took in a cargo but on her return, after scarcely two hours at sea, we fell in with two King's cutters, which had been sent to look for us. They were the *Stork* under Captain Amos [Thomas Amos], and the *Swallow* under Captain Ferris [William Ferris].

As soon as we perceived them, we veered off toward France, but finding that this manoeuvre would not do, we altered course for England. An arduous chase then ensued, and for a long time the result was in doubt, but at about 6 o'clock in the evening, despite our utmost efforts, the *Swallow* came up with us. About a third of a league behind her was the *Stork*, picking up the tubs which we had thrown overboard.

As soon as the *Swallow* came alongside everyone - except myself and two others - got in our boat, rowed off in her, and made their escape. I and my companions were taken on board the *Swallow*. The captain asked me for my papers, which I gave him. He then went off in his boat to the other cutter. He returned soon afterwards with Captain Amos, who took me on board the *Stork* with him. He was a man of courteous manners therefore, although I was a smuggler and his prisoner, he behaved towards me with great kindness, and even invited me into his cabin where I both ate and drank with him.

The next day, having picked up our tubs, they proceeded to Weymouth roads. There my companions [ie from the smuggling boat] sent a friend off in a boat with a letter for me, but the captain of the *Stork* would not allow it to be delivered. He ordered me below.

At dawn the next morning, the two cutters with their prize set out for Cowes. Soon after our arrival, a lieutenant and his gang came on board.

"Rattenbury," the captain said to me, "I am going to send you on board a man-of-war, and you must get clear how you can."

"Sir," I replied, "you have been giving me roast meat ever since I came aboard and now you have run the spit into me."

Rattenbury's smuggling boat was a three-masted lugger called *Brothers*, built in Beer in 1807. The official owner was Abraham Mutter, a Burton Bradstock shipwright. She was captured by the two Cowes cutters on 11 May 1808 with 135 small casks of spirits aboard. A report at Cowes gives the captain of the *Swallow* as Amos, and the captain of the *Stork* as Ferris. *Brothers* was condemned for illicit trading. Its registration was cancelled on 28 March 1809 and it was broken up at Cowes. The reward for Amos and Ferris - their moiety on the sale of the spirits and the boat's materials - came to £71 each.

The *Brothers* first master was William Farrant, the same man Rattenbury succeeded on the *Trafalgar*. Rattenbury replaced him on the *Brothers* on 21 April 1808, two weeks before her fateful encounter with the *Swallow* and *Stork*.

There appear to have been two Abraham Mutters involved with Rattenbury, although reading his account you would never guess there was even one! There was Abraham Mutter of Burton Bradstock, and there was Abraham Mutter of Seaton and Beer, who is reputed to have been Rattenbury's partner for many years.

A prisoner again, Rattenbury found himself once more aboard the guard ship *Royal William*.

I was put on board the *Royal William*, the ship from which I had escaped before. There I found a great many smugglers, and although I was acquainted with them, none of the officers seemed to have any recollection of me, though I was on board for a fortnight.

Soon after, I and all the other smugglers were drafted on board the *Resistance* frigate under Captain Adams. The next evening we set sail from Portsmouth bound for Ireland. After eight days at sea, we arrived at Cork. I thought that it was high time I formed a plan to regain my liberty so, after being there four days, I enlisted the aid of an Irish bumboat-man [a bumboat ferried goods and supplies from shore to a ship at anchor in order to sell them to those on board]. I engaged him to come to the ship's buoy where I would swim off to him, promising that if he got me safe on shore, I would give him seven guineas.

The man was punctual, but the marines were keeping such a strict look-out, I could not accomplish my design. Seeing little prospect of being able to do so, I determined to keep my eyes open, and to seize an opportunity to get clear in some other way.

The next day was Tuesday and the ship's launch came alongside to take in casks for the purpose of getting water. While the first lieutenant was scolding a midshipman for not being quick enough getting them on board, I jumped in the boat. With a cask before me, I took up an oar and assisted with others in rowing to the shore. When we got there, another boat was taking in water. This caused a delay so the midshipman said he would take us all to a public-house and get some whiskey. I got out with the rest, but stole away unperceived by anyone.

I ran four miles into the country where I fell in with a very civil and kind-hearted woman to whom I disclosed as much of my story as I deemed necessary. She took me to a farm house where I was treated very hospitably. The farmer sent his son to the Cove of Cork to collect all the news he could. When the son returned, he said that the whole place was in a kind of alarm because the captain of the smugglers had escaped, and that marine officers and their men had been searching every public-house with a view to apprehending me and bringing me back.

Upon receiving this intelligence, I hired a gig that same evening, and set out for Youghal, where I arrived at day-break. I then went to the harbour to enquire about a vessel for England, and had the good fortune to find one bound for Weymouth. I went on board and met the mate, who introduced me to the captain. The captain had a brother who was a fellow-smuggler, one with whom I had long been acquainted, so we soon came to an agreement.

The captain behaved kindly towards me, and that same day I went and dined with him and all the masters of the vessels that were also there. Two officers of the royal navy were of the party. Three hours we spent together, me passing for the captain of a vessel.

The same evening we set sail and, after being at sea three days, got off Start Point where the captain put me on board a boat bound for Brixham. At Brixham I found another boat from Beer and so I arrived there safe at 4 o'clock on Sunday morning, to the great joy of myself, my wife, and family. From escape at Cork, it had taken me six days to get home.

At home was Anna and their two children, William and Frances, aged six and three respectively.

At no point in his narrative does Rattenbury make a direct reference to the *Friendship*, the square-sterned cutter of which he was master for two years, from November 1808 to November 1810. Built in Sidmouth in February 1807, she was sold to Lyme sailmaker William Troy in November 1808, which is when Rattenbury took over. It was surely the *Friendship* he planned to use in his next highly irregular venture?

Not long after my return home I made an agreement with four French officers, who had escaped from the prison at Tiverton. I was to take them to Cape La Hogue, for which I was to receive £100. They came to Beer and I concealed them in a house near the beach, where I supplied them with such provisions as they wanted. However, a vigilant enquiry had commenced, their steps were traced, and the place of their retreat discovered.

The next morning, a special warrant was issued against myself as captain of the boat, and five others connected with the affair. The constables came to my house while I was upstairs considering how best to act. My companions had absconded. I surrendered myself and was taken before the magistrates. There I found the French gentlemen in custody. They were examined through an interpreter, but their replies were cautious and they said very little that would implicate me in the transaction.

My turn then came and, in reply to the questions from the bench, I briefly stated that I had been engaged to take the gentlemen to Jersey, of which island I understood they were natives. A lieutenant of the sea-fencibles was in the room.

"Don't you know a native of Jersey from a Frenchman?" he asked me.

I would have replied but my attorney, who was present, said that he had no right to ask the question and therefore I did not have to answer it. The magistrates conferred and, after a little consultation, dismissed me with a gentle admonition to go home and not engage in a similar transaction in the future.

As England had been at war with France on and off since 1793, there was a large number of French nationals either imprisoned in England or living in parole towns like Tiverton. According to Emily Skinner in an article in *Devon Notes & Queries*, Vol IV, Tiverton housed what she describes as 'a better class of prisoner', many of them 'of good social position'. Between 1797 and 1811 no less than 1000 Frenchmen (and some women and children) passed through the formal charge of the town's mayor. Being on parole, they received many liberties and privileges denied to other prisoners, but there were restrictions. They had to return to their lodgings when the curfew bell was rung at St George's Church, and none were allowed more than a mile out of town. Once a week they had to sign their names in a register kept at the town clerk's office. Emily Skinner says that:

> "The prisoners made themselves useful and agreeable during their stay, and employed their time in skilful workmanship - in carving and inlaid Sheraton work, some in the form of small grandfather's clocks for the turnip watch then in vogue. They instructed the inhabitants in the use of herbs, and taught them French preparations of vegetables, but Tiverton people were never reconciled to their habit of collecting and cooking snails."

Some prisoners were repatriated to France, and a few escaped, but not the four Rattenbury tried to help. The tolerance of the magistrates towards a man caught trying to smuggle out of England - for personal profit - some of the nation's enemies seems rather surprising.

The lieutenant - or rather the captain - of the sea-fencibles Rattenbury refers to is the same man who features in the next part of his story - Durell. In early 1807, Captain Durell filed one of the many reports sent to the Exeter collector about smuggling in the Beer area, so by November 1808 Rattenbury would have been well known to him.

A short time later, Lt Durell of the sea-fencibles went to my house with constables to apprehend me as a deserter from His Majesty's navy. I happened to see them go in. Guessing the object of their visit, I made my escape round the cliffs. I stayed away from home until I judged that this storm - which threatened to destroy my domestic peace - had blown over.

15. Dolphin Hotel, Beer

Soon after, I bought a vessel for smuggling and made three successful voyages to Alderney in it. On my return from the last, thinking all was safe, I went on shore with a few friends to spend an hour at a public-house. In the same room was Sergeant Hill and several privates belonging to the South Devon militia, and some horse-soldiers [dragoons]. There were about nine or ten in all.

The public-house in which Hill and his militiamen, the dragoons, and Rattenbury were all drinking was in Beer, in which case it may have been the *Dolphin Inn*, the *Anchor Inn,* or perhaps the *New Inn.*

The South Devon militia was the force which Lord Rolle had commanded in Ireland in 1799. The militia and the local sea fencibles may have been different military organisations which Rattenbury confused by interchanging their names. Having specifically referred to Durell as being of the sea fencibles, Rattenbury now implies that he was in charge of the local militiamen.

> After drinking two or three pots of beer, Sergeant Hill, having heard my companions mention my name, went out with his men, and having armed themselves with swords and muskets, they came back in again. The sergeant came toward me.
>
> "You are my prisoner," he said. "You are a deserter and must come with me."
>
> For a moment I was terrified because I knew that if I was taken, I would have to go through the fleet.

The naval punishment for desertion was three hundred lashes of a cat o'nine tails, delivered 25 at a time in front of the crew of every ship in the fleet, the deserter being ferried around in a launch for the purpose. It was not unusual for the man to die, therefore Rattenbury's desperation in seeking to avoid such a terrible flogging is by no means exaggerated.

> The thought made me desperate although I tried to appear as cool as possible.
>
> "Sergeant," I replied, "you are surely labouring under an error. I have done nothing that gives you the authority to take me up, or detain me. You have mistaken me for someone else."
>
> While I was parleying with him in this manner I jumped into the cellar, throwing off my jacket and shirt to prevent anyone from using them to hold me. Having armed myself with a reap hook, and with the knife I had in my pocket, I threw myself into an attitude of defence at the cellar's entrance. It was a half-hatch door, the lower part being shut.
>
> "I won't be taken from this spot alive!" I declared. "I'll kill the first man who comes near me!"
>
> At this, the sergeant was evidently terrified. "Soldiers," he said to his men, "do your duty. Advance and seize him!"
>
> "Sergeant," they replied, "you proposed it, so you take the lead. Set us an example, and we will follow."

But he didn't. No-one offered to advance and there I remained, holding them at bay for four hours. Not knowing how to act, the sergeant at last sent for Lt Durell. Before he arrived, a woman ran into the house saying a vessel had drifted ashore and that a boy was in danger of being drowned. The tale was told in such a natural manner that it attracted the attention of the sergeant and his men. While they were listening, and making enquiries about it, I jumped over the hatch and pushed through their midst. None could get a hold on me because I had taken the precaution of laying aside my clothes.

I ran towards the beach, and some men got me into a boat and conveyed me on board my vessel, where I immediately hoisted the colours. When Lt Durell came down to the beach and saw the colours flying, he asked why.

"It's only a freak of Rattenbury's," some bystanders replied. "He has escaped from the soldiers and has raised them in triumph."

Upon hearing this Lt Durell flew into a great rage and told his soldiers that if they took me and brought me to him then, as well as the deserting money, he would give them two guineas out of his own pocket. But I made sure I stayed on board. A friend advised me to put into Lyme. He said he would keep a sharp look-out, and would always inform me if I was likely to be in danger.

I then made a voyage to Alderney. I was there and back in two days and saved the cargo. I made other voyages too, with similar success, but I preferred to put into Lyme, as I had several good friends there.

Not only good friends - the owner of his vessel lived there too; so did members of his wife's family.

Early one morning, having slept the night at Lyme, I went down to see how the vessel lay because I was apprehensive about the weather. Looking around, I saw that the sky was very dark and angry. There was every appearance of a heavy gale coming on. Suddenly I heard the report of a gun, and then another. I jumped upon a wall to get a wider view and saw a brig in the offing. She had her colours up as a signal of distress.

I got a boat, and three men, and put off to her. She was the *Linskill* [*Linskel*] transport, and on board was part of the 82nd Regiment and several officers.

As we came alongside, the captain said he was a stranger to the coast, and they were in danger of losing the vessel. He begged us to take them into some harbour. I said I would do everything in my power to save them. We went on board and I asked the captain what water he drew. It was 22 feet. I told him I could not take them into Lyme as it was then neap tides, and the gale was rapidly coming on. The officers entreated me not to leave them, but to take the vessel into some other port. Just then another transport vessel came into the bay and came close to us, so we sent a boat to her with directions to keep close after us. We made all the canvass we could and got clear.

Outside Portland, we fell in with an East Indiaman, which also asked for assistance because the gale was so violent, but we were unable to afford them any. We never learned her fate.

Through the goodness of Divine Providence, we at last weathered this tremendous storm. The danger over, the grateful officers were so profuse in their acknowledgements of the service I had rendered, that I ventured to tell them about the trouble I was in, and how my enemies were in search of me. They heard me with attention and I asked their advice. They said that, as soon as we got ashore, I should get printed a hand-bill, describing what I had done in their behalf. They even presented me with a guinea to defray the expense.

I guided the transport into the Needles where she took another pilot. At our parting the captain gave me twenty guineas for my pilotage and I left the vessel with the highest commendation of the officers and crew, and their best wishes for my future prosperity and success.

As soon as I got on shore, I went to a printer and had a hand-bill struck off, which was to be of great use to me. I then went home. However, I was so fearful of being apprehended, and of encountering trouble, that I did not venture abroad.

About three weeks after my return, Lord Rolle and his lady came to Beer to visit a charity school, of which they were the benefactors. When we heard about it my wife followed them and presented one of my hand-bills to his lordship. She begged him to read it, which he did, with considerable attention. As he went down the street he said that he would do something for me. An hour later he returned.

"Where is the good woman who was speaking to me about her husband?" he said to someone nearby.

My wife advanced. His lordship saw her. "I am sorry, I can't do anything for your husband because I have been informed that he is the man who threatened to cut my sergeant's guts out."

When I heard of this, I ran after her ladyship, who had quitted the village. I overtook her carriage, fell down on my knees, and presented one of my hand-bills, entreating her to use her influence with his lordship on my behalf, to stop the sergeant taking me.

"You have such spirits for fighting, you ought to go back on board a man-or-war," she said, "and be equal to Lord Nelson. If you do so, I will take care that you shall not he hurt, depend on it."

"My lady," I replied. "I have always had an aversion to the navy. I wish to remain with my wife and family, and to support them in a creditable manner, and therefore can never think of returning."

Her ladyship then said, "I will consider it," and turned off.

About a week later, the soldiers were ordered away from Beer, I believe through the influence of her ladyship and the humanity of Lord Rolle.

It was on 24 January 1809 that Rattenbury helped the *Linskel*. The men of the 82nd regiment were returning from Spain and the Peninsular War. The hand-bill Rattenbury had printed was published in the *Exeter Flying Post* on 9 February 1809:

> *"This is to certify that John Raddenbury, pilot, of Beer, near Axminster, was of great service to the brig* Linskel *Transport, in assisting her out of a perilous situation on the 24th instant, by getting on board her off Lyme; and saved her from foundering off Abbotsbury Beach, having on board part of the 82nd Regiment of Foot, from Spain. Witness: Major McDonell, Capt G Marshall, etc. Dated January 26 1809."*

Lady Rolle was Judith Maria Walrond, one of the Walronds of Bovey House which she brought to Lord Rolle as part of her dowry. Bovey House was situated close to Beer hence her continuing interest in the communities in the neighbourhood. She died in 1820. Two years later Lord Rolle married Lady Louisa Trefusis.

It had been a bold move petitioning Lord Rolle, who commanded the militia, but it seems to have worked for Rattenbury no longer felt any fear of arrest for desertion.

> I felt a great weight removed from my mind. I was freed from the fears that had so long haunted my walks by day, and my pillow by night. I would gladly have entered on a new course of life, but I found myself entangled with difficulties from which I was unable to escape, being bound by a chain of circumstances whose links I was unable to break.
>
> Accordingly, I went to Alderney and took in a cargo, but returning home we were overtaken by foul weather. About three leagues off from land we lost our mast in a gale of wind, but saved our rigging by means of a tackle. We fell in with a Brixham fishing boat, and gave the master thirty guineas to tow us into that port. This was in January 1809.
>
> In the following July I went to Dartmouth and bought a vessel called the *Lively*, which we afterwards sold to pay for the repairs of the other.
>
> I now seriously resolved to abandon the trade of smuggling.

So often Rattenbury refers to 'we' without telling his readers who he was referring to. In this case the generalisation surely includes Beer mariner William Westlake, his partner in the ownership of the *Lively* since November 1807.

CHAPTER 11

Publican, Pilot, and Fisherman
1809-1814

Rattenbury says he resolved to give up smuggling, but the truth is that, in 1809, smuggling gave him up. By a mixture of design (the establishment of customs outports on Jersey and Guernsey in 1807 which gradually closed the Channel Islands as a market for the purchase of contraband), and coincidence (the outbreak of the Peninsular War with France in 1808 which closed the alternative markets in French ports such as Cherbourg and Roscoff), smuggling came to a virtual standstill. Merchants like Robilliard in Weymouth went out of business, and smugglers like Rattenbury had little option but to seek other employment.

> I decided to take a public-house and use my leisure hours to fish. At first, the public house appeared to suit me pretty well, but after being in it for two years I discovered that I had gone back in the world considerably. My circumstances, instead of improving, were daily getting worse, because all the money I could get by fishing and piloting was going to the brewer with whom the business was confined.

Rattenbury does not say where his public-house was located, but there is no reason to suppose it was anywhere but Beer. Both of the children born during his period - John Partridge in October 1809, and Ann in December 1812 - were baptised in Beer. We do not know the name of his public-house. He never describes it as an inn, so it may not have been the *Dolphin, Anchor,* or *New Inn,* but a 'pot-house', as the Rev. Swete designated such establishments in 1794.

> Times were then very hard, with trade and commerce being in a state of great stagnation and with little or no prospect of their revival. Not knowing what else to do, I returned to my old trade of smuggling.
> In November 1812 I went in a vessel to Alderney. Returning home, at day-break, about half way across the Channel, we fell in with one of His Majesty's cruisers, the *Catherine* brig, commanded by Captain Tingle. A warm chase ensued, in the course of which she fired 24 cannon shot at us. We were considerably alarmed because, at the time, we did not know what she was, and thought she might be a French privateer. At about half-past ten in the morning they came so near to us that, finding there was no hope of escaping, we hauled down all our sails. But the crew kept up an incessant fire of small arms upon us,

several of which went through our binnacle and bulwarks, and through the sails we had hauled down.

All the men, except myself, were below, yet despite this tremendous volley I escaped without a single wound. I have since reflected on that circumstance, and not without wonder, but my mind was then in such a state of excitement that I thought little of the danger I was exposed to.

"You rascals!" the captain called out when he came within hail of us. "I'll put you all on board a man-of-war!" He inspected the vessel, but to his great disappointment found nothing on board except a pint of gin in a bottle. He still detained our vessel, and putting myself and my companions on board his own brig, he took us into Brixham.

When we arrived I asked him if I could go on shore, but he peremptorily refused. He himself went off in a boat, charging his men to take particular care of us. I was not disheartened and decided to make another application, so on his return to the brig I went below to him and renewed my request. I met with another denial.

"You have behaved towards me most shamefully," I then said to him. "You took my vessel on the high seas, and though you found nothing on board to justify your action, you detained it, therefore it is an act of piracy."

"I care nothing about it," he replied. "You have given me a great deal of trouble, and I will not let you go on shore unless I receive orders to that effect from the Board."

As she was convoy to the Brixham fishermen [to protect them from French privateers], the *Catherine* brig went to sea again the next day, with us on board. We went cruising for about a week. When she came into the bay again, I repeated my request to the captain, but with no better success than before. As he stepped over the side of the vessel to go on shore, he told the crew to keep a sharp look-out. He said that if one of us escaped, one of them should suffer in his stead.

My wife had heard of my situation, and that same day she, and the wives of my companions, came on board. Our interview was short, but long enough for me to entreat her to get a good boat and to come off to me the next morning. In the evening, I explained part of my plan to my companions, and told them to be ready to act according to the hints I gave. It was about 10 o'clock in the morning when my wife came.

The only way the following incident makes sense is if you accept that Anna Rattenbury and the other wives get *out* of the boat they bring to the brig, in order to allow their menfolk to get *in*, the men then getting away *without* them.

The other officers being on shore, the second mate had charge of the vessel, a circumstance favourable to my design. As soon as my wife and the other females were alongside, I jumped into the boat and motioned to my companions to do the same, so that we could help them on board. One did so. I whispered to him to wait till they were all out of the boat. As soon as this was accomplished, I called out aloud, "Shove off!" upon which three other of my companions jumped in.

I put my oar against the side of the vessel, but the second mate caught hold of it and broke off the blade. Angrily, I threw the remaining part at him. I called to my companions to hoist the sail.

"If you do, I'll fire at you!" he warned.

"Make sure of your mark!" I replied.

At this he fired. The shot went through the sails. He was preparing to fire again when my wife wrested the piece out of his hands. He recovered it and fired again. The shot struck the sail rope and it fell down. Thinking we were sufficiently terrified to be induced to return to the ship, he stopped firing, but by then we had hoisted our sail again, and pushed off. They then got their boat out and chased us, keeping up a continual fire but, though the sails were full of shot-holes, none of our men received any injury.

We put in at a promontory called Bob's nose [Hope's nose?]. My companions jumped out. Having steered the boat, I was the last. As I got out a shot passed close to my head.

Once ashore I scrambled up the cliffs. When I had reached the top, I looked back. I could see no-one. I took off my jacket, dropped it, then rolled back down the cliff not far from where we landed. I thought that if they found the jacket they would suppose I had thrown it off to facilitate my speed in getting away. I saw our pursuers following my companions. On Brixham hills several hundred people looked on, but too far off to give the least assistance.

It was now about 11 o'clock. I was without hat or jacket, and the rain was descending in torrents. Among the rocks I found the best retreat I could and remained there until 4 o'clock in the afternoon.

About one, I had seen the men belonging to the brig go by and embark so, when all seemed quiet, I started over hedges, fields, and ditches, and got to Torquay. I went to a public house kept by a friend where I got dry clothes and refreshment. I then sent a man and horse to my wife and directed her to meet me the next day.

The following morning I received a letter informing me that two of my companions had been retaken. When my wife arrived, she told me they had both been sentenced to go on board a man-of-war bound for the West Indies. We then set off together and got home safe to Beer.

We remained in the public house until November 1813 when, in consequence of bad debts, several misfortunes, and the general stagnation of trade at that period, we shut it up. We were unable to carry it on any longer.

My situation was now deplorable for I had a wife and four children [William 11, Frances 8, John 4, and Ann 1] to support. My money was all gone, and there was scarcely anything to be done in smuggling. I had nothing left but a boat, in which I and my eldest son used to go fishing. This was how we were employed during the summer [of 1814?], although we met with indifferent success.

In the fall of the same year, another calamity overtook us. We were fishing when a gale of wind came on, sending us towards the shore. Before we reached it, a very heavy sea broke over the boat and she was shattered to pieces. It was only with difficulty that we escaped with our lives.

All my hopes were now destroyed. I had lost everything and, what with winter coming on, we were very disconsolate. Fortunately, things were not as bad as we thought for two vessels were driven into the bay by stress of weather, and I was engaged in piloting them. As I was paid handsomely for this, my domestic troubles were not only lightened, but I was able to pay £10 to the spirit merchant with whom I was in arrears when I left the public house.

One of John Rattenbury's rivals in dispensing alcohol to the locals was James Holmes, who is described in the Parish register of 1813 as an inn-keeper. Perhaps it was he who kept the *Dolphin Inn*? But who was this 'spirit merchant' to whom Rattenbury became indebted? In 1814, a Samuel Hammett was a local vintner. Was it him? In 1817, Hammett was described as a master smuggler by local customs officers who caught him lighting fires to warn off a smuggling boat.

The parish records of Beer and Seaton at this time reveal that most of the fathers who had their children baptised were either mariners (fishermen or seamen), or labourers, but there was the usual smattering of tradesmen - a shopkeeper, butcher, cordwainer, carpenter, barber, a couple of masons and, of course, several customs officers.

Since 1807 some of the customs personnel at Beer had changed, but not all. In 1814 the boatmen were John Peek (senior boatman), John and Peter Gibbs, George Mills, Samuel Freeman and David Sterling - six men for a six-oared boat. The sitter was John Curtis. In order to supplement their wages, the boatmen were allowed to offer themselves as pilots. On one notable occasion the Beer boatmen did so, only to find themselves in fierce competition with John Rattenbury:

In January 1814, I was on the look-out on the cliffs near Beer when I spied a vessel about two leagues off to the southward. I saw, by means of my glass, that she was a Dutch galliot and in danger of becoming a wreck. I immediately procured a boat and some men and went off to her to render assistance, but a custom house boat, which was also on the look-out, saw me and got to the vessel first.

When I got on board, I found that in order to make sure of the job, they were offering to take her into port for £30. I told the captain that they knew little about pilotage and had no right to undertake it, so he said he would employ me and have nothing to do with them. When they heard this, the custom house men agreed that I should do it, and that I should allow them their share of the £30.

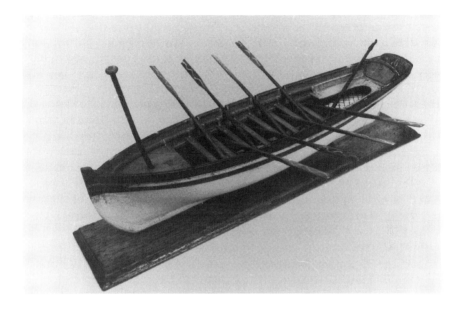

16. Model of 18th-19th Century rowing boat

"What would you do it for?" the captain then asked me. "Do you agree to the proposition they have made?"

I replied that I would give them their share of the sum as they had proposed, or settle the matter by arbitration afterwards, but that I could not undertake to put the vessel into Brixham - the port he wished to go to - for less than £100. These terms were mutually agreed and, having rigged a jury mast [ie a temporary mast], I piloted the vessel safe into Brixham that same afternoon.

In the evening I waited on the agent. He told me to call on him the next day for the money, as that was the agreement. I did. As soon as I received it, I satisfied the men I had employed for their assistance, and then gave the custom officers their proportion of the sum they had fixed upon. But they were not content with this and put in a claim for a full share of the £100. Their demand was extortionate and unjust and I refused to comply with it, therefore they summoned me to appear before the magistrates.

A minute investigation took place. I was put on oath, after which the customs men acknowledged that what I said accorded with their agreement. On being asked how they could expect any more, they had nothing to say for themselves and the magistrates dismissed the case, sending them about their business. However, because of this they were continually annoying me, overhauling my bags and other things, in the hope of finding smuggled articles, with a view to injuring myself and my family.

A short time after, the sitter of the boat - who was my greatest enemy - was taken off in a very sudden and awful manner, for as he was riding along the road near Seaton, he fell from his horse, and pitching forward on his face into a small stream of water about four inches deep, was drowned.

John Curtis, the Beer sitter, did not drown in a stream. He died at his home on the morning of 1 October 1816. What is not clear is what he died of, whether it was from injuries he had sustained, or an illness. That he was brought fatally low in a very short time is indisputable because, only two weeks earlier, in full possession of his faculties, he had replied at length to an enquiry from the Lyme collector about the conduct of one of his men. But there is no suspicion of foul play which, given Rattenbury's account, and his animosity towards Curtis, one might have expected. When on 29 September, Richard Broadbridge, the Seaton riding officer, visited Curtis at his home, he described the sitter as being 'on his death-bed' but 'perfectly sensible'. When Curtis died, senior boatman John Peek was appointed to take his place.

The intense competition for work between seamen like Rattenbury and the Beer boatmen was probably due to the persistent recessionary influences of the Peninsular War which, in January 1814, was in its final stages.

At the beginning of 1814 trade was extremely dull because of the fluctuating nature of our public affairs. Smuggling was also at a standstill. However, I was always on the look-out because I had a large family, so when I heard that Mr Downe, a gentleman then residing at Bridport, wanted a person to rig a vessel and go fishing for him, I immediately went to see him and offered to undertake the job. He made some enquiries, found that I was capable of doing it, and agreed to employ myself and my son [William, then 12] on very liberal terms.

We went to Bridport where we were engaged in this work from February till the end of April, when the vessel was ready for sea. Mr Downe then paid myself and my son at the rate of 27 shillings per week for our joint labour, and discharged our bill at the public-house where we had lodged during the whole time we were employed on it.

We went fishing in the vessel until July, and were paid by the share. We found, however, that this speculation would not answer because Bridport was an inconvenient place to go in and out at. Our employer ordered the vessel to be laid up, and we went home again.

This engagement proved a great relief to my circumstances for, as I said, every other kind of trade was very dead.

17. West Bay, Bridport

In the second half of the 18th Century, the Downes were one of the leading families in Bridport. William Downe 1744-1820, was the most notable, being both a ship-owner in Bridport and a merchant in London, where he had a wharf. In about 1789, he built in Bridport a replica of his London home, calling it Downe Hall. A Nathaniel Downe was bailiff of Bridport several times between 1807 and 1816. Unfortunately there are no clues in Rattenbury's narrative as to which Downe it was that hired him and his son to go fishing.

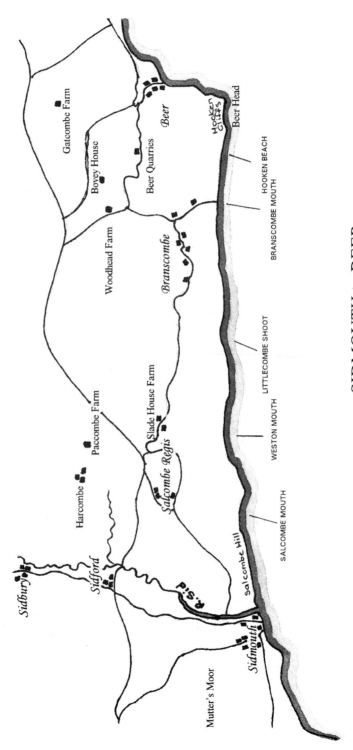

SIDMOUTH to BEER

CHAPTER 12

Smuggling around Lyme and Sidmouth 1814-1816

The Peninsular War came to an end in April 1814 with the defeat and exile of Napoleon Bonaparte. After the cessation of hostilities, French ports were re-opened to English merchants. English smugglers, no longer able to buy foreign spirits from the Channel Islands, sailed instead to Cherbourg and Roscoff for their purchases. French merchants and fishermen began to co-operate with the smugglers - preparing the goods for the purpose, and hiring out vessels and men to carry them to the coast of England - just as the Channel Islanders had done.

In August of the same year [1814], out of the money which I received of Mr Downe, I bought another boat. In it I went fishing a few times but, as Cherbourg was open for smuggling, I took my son [William 12], and two men, and went there for that purpose. Our first voyage took a fortnight to complete, but we landed all safely. It proved so profitable that it set me up in the world again, and revived all my ardour for speculation.

Having some business to transact, I stayed home for its second voyage, which was completed successfully in ten days. For the third, I again remained on shore, sending a man in my place. On their return, the men sunk the goods, but when they landed the tidewaiter seized the boat, which we lost, although the cargo was saved.

One Beer vessel lost to customs at this time was the *Flora*, seized by riding officer Richard Broadbridge on Seaton beach on 18 November 1814. He subsequently submitted a bill for the amount it cost him to get the boat to the Custom House in Lyme:

"Expenses for horses and cart in removing the masts and sails of the boat Flora, *seized on the beach at Seaton for being concerned in smuggling - 6 shillings. Two men and labour etc in assisting - 4 shillings. Store room for the materials - 5 shillings.*

21 November. Horse and Waggon for removing the above to Seaton Hole and hauling the boat to the waterside - 10 shillings; launching and taking the same to the King's Warehouse at Lyme - 15 shillings." (PRO. Lyme Letterbooks CUST 63/1)

From 1814 to the end of 1816, Rattenbury operated between Lyme Regis in the east and Sidmouth in the west, avoiding Beer as much as possible because there John Curtis and his boatmen were keeping a close eye on him. For that same reason, he sometimes chose to stay at home and send others to Cherbourg in his stead.

> In September [1814] I went to Cherbourg with three other persons, in a boat belonging to another man. On our return we sunk the goods, and landed all safely.
>
> In November, I went back to Cherbourg and we took in a cargo, but coming back in company with two other smuggling boats, we were overtaken by a most tremendous gale, which obliged us to sink our goods and run ashore. The next day, the officers seized the boats. The morning after that the custom house boat ran over our buoy and took up all the kegs, 100 of them, which was a severe loss.

According to Clive Hardy in *The Smuggler's Guide to Purbeck*, cork floats were sometimes used by smugglers to mark the place where a cargo was sunk. When the goods were to be retrieved, a grappling hook was dropped over the side of the recovery vessel and dragged along to catch up the tubs. The same method was used by customs boatmen when they went fishing for smuggled contraband. It obviously helped if the officers had a rough idea where the tubs had been sunk. In this case, they probably did, but one gets the feeling that, between 1814 and 1816, so many tubs were being sunk off the Devon coast that routine creeping may not have been a waste of time!

> In the latter end of September [1814] I went to Cherbourg with two other men where, by appointment, we met a Frenchman. He lent us his vessel for one voyage, for which we agreed to give him £25. We loaded her up and put to sea, but a gale of wind detained us in the Channel for three days. The vessel was so leaky, we sunk our goods, and put into Lyme Cobb. A few days later the weather became calm, and we went for our goods, which we got on shore without meeting with any interruption.
>
> In January 1815, with another man, I went again to Cherbourg in a vessel which we hired. Our voyage, which lasted fourteen days, was troublesome. On our return, we arrived at an open beach and were on the point of landing, when a signal from our friends put us off. Revenue officers and soldiers were on the look-out, so we sunk our goods. We had no opportunity of retrieving them for nearly three weeks. During that time the weather was so frosty that when we did take them up, the spirits had become thick. They were so much injured in quality, that we were obliged to sell them for what we could get.
>
> I remained on shore till March [1815], when I bought half a boat. With two other men, I again went to Cherbourg. The voyage lasted six days, and we landed safe and well.

In October [1815], with another man, I went to Exmouth, where we bought a vessel called the *Volante* for £200. We took her into Lyme to have her bowsprit stemmed, then went smuggling in her. She was very leaky but we continued to make good voyages in her all winter.

The *Volante*, built in Seaton in 1803, was re-registered at Lyme on 6 November 1815 under the ownership of Lyme mariner William Dominy. Her master was William Puttam. Rattenbury's early voyages in her were from Dominy's base at Lyme because of the surveillance he was under at home.

Rattenbury and his colleagues were not the only smugglers John Curtis and his boatmen had to contend with. In the autumn of 1815, they filed report after report at the Custom House in Lyme. In the early hours of 29 October, they were keeping watch at various places on the coast near Beer when, at about 2am, John Peek and George Mills saw three men carrying tubs. They were coming up from the beach at Seaton Hole. As soon as the men saw the officers, they threw down their burdens and ran off. By the time Peek and Mills had collected the tubs, the boat which had landed them had put to sea again.

At 3am the same morning, John Curtis was at the top of the hills between Beer and Branscombe when he too saw a man with a tub on his back. The man saw him, threw down the tub, and called out a warning. That was when Curtis saw even more men, all running in different directions. Searching around he found the tub the man had dropped, and another hidden in the hedge.

Curtis's opposite number in Bridport, which was also under the jurisdiction of the collector at Lyme, was Thomas Jarvis. It was not unusual for former captains to become senior boatmen in the preventive service, therefore it is perfectly feasible that this was the same Thomas Jarvis who had been master of the *Friends* in 1798.

On the night of 26 October, Jarvis and his boatmen were on the look-out at Chideock. It was very dark and it was raining. At 11pm they heard footsteps. Convinced it was smugglers, they ran towards the shore but the smugglers, aware of their presence, had dispersed. Jarvis and his men searched the beach but found nothing. They placed themselves at various places as sentinels in order to prevent anything being carried off, and at daylight searched the cliffs. They found nine casks.

At Lyme itself, where there were five tidewaiters (John Wood, Thomas Lock, John Freeman, Joseph Cox and Abraham Mills), and two boatmen (William Clarke and William Wood), the smugglers were just as active. At midnight on 29 September, John Freeman was on the look-out on the shore near the harbour when he saw two men, who appeared to have casks on their backs. He watched, and saw them hide the casks away. Immediately afterwards, four other men, each with two casks, appeared and deposited their burdens in the same spot. They went towards the shore and, in a short time, returned with six more casks. Freeman approached the men who threw the casks from their backs and ran off, leaving him with a total of sixteen, which he conveyed the next morning to the Custom House.

Boatmen and tidewaiters usually watched the coast, leaving the activities of smugglers further inland to the riding officers. In this duty the Seaton riding officer, Richard Broadbridge, was frequently aided by coastwaiter George Gerhard, who lived in Beer. Although both were attached to Exeter outport, their seizures were sometimes recorded at Lyme. Their reports from 1815 give a remarkable insight into the aspects of local smuggling completely absent from Rattenbury's account, notably how the contraband was conveyed inland from the beach on the night it was landed, and where some of it was stored. Smugglers caught carrying the contraband are named and some were later prosecuted before magistrates.

On the night of 29 September 1815, Broadbridge and Gerhard were on the look-out for smugglers, moving from place to place as the night progressed. At 3am they went towards Colyton Hill where they heard noises of men passing over a hedge. Going to the spot, they discovered a man carrying a keg. He was about to go through a hedge. Investigating, they saw that two other men, also carrying kegs, had

18. *Seaton Bay 1829*

preceded him. When the three men saw the officers, they threw down their kegs and ran off in different directions. Broadbridge left Gerhard in charge of the contraband, and pursued them, but failed to catch them. He returned to Gerhard and they stayed with their seizure until dawn when they made a thorough search of the area, They found two more kegs in the ditch of a field belonging to Thomas Holmes, described as a noted smuggler, who lived at Gatcombe Farm, near Colyton. These they also seized.

A month later, on the evening of 30 October 1815, Gerhard and Broadbridge were again on a tour of duty. They separated. Soon after Gerhard met James Farrant, a Seaton shoemaker and known smuggler. The encounter took place very close to Seaton Chan, where a boat was unloading contraband. Farrant, realising that Gerhard was not a fellow smuggler, cried 'Look out!', the signal smugglers used when they discovered customs officers. Having foiled Gerhard's seizure, Farrant ran towards the sea. Gerhard consulted with Broadbridge and they decided that, as the goods had been unloaded at Seaton Chan, the smugglers might take their usual route inland and therefore the officers had a chance of intercepting them. They therefore went across the fields to Gatcombe Farm.

Again the two officers separated. Gerhard encountered three men on foot, one carrying two casks on his shoulders and two carrying one each. When Gerhard ordered them to stop they threw down their casks and ran off. Gerhard pursued them and caught one. He was John Lloyd, a servant living with that same Thomas Holmes on whose land they had seized two tubs a month earlier. Gerhard saw other men coming up the road towards Gatcombe and he went forward but, the alarm given, they made off before he could discover if they were carrying casks.

There seems little doubt from the reports filed by Gerhard and Broadbridge, that on both 29 September and 30 October, Gatcombe Farm was the destination of the contraband landed on the coast near Seaton, and there it would have been stored - almost certainly with the knowledge of Thomas Holmes - until it could be sold or transported onwards. A year later, on 20 December 1816, the same two customs men found eleven casks in a barn belonging to Holmes but he could not be prosecuted because they could not prove he knew they were there.

The smugglers did not always use Seaton Chan. On 21 October 1816, Broadbridge and Gerhard, having met by appointment in Beer, spotted a smuggling vessel to the westward and followed it to Weston Mouth, where the smugglers were warned off, probably by the lighting of fires on land. The vessel then went on to Salcombe beach where one man with one cask was landed. He was also a lookout, and when he saw the two customs men, he threw his cask into the furze and shouted a warning to the others, causing the boat to put to sea again.

As it was moonlight, the officers could see the boat making for Sidmouth beach so they made for Sidmouth too, reaching it at about 4am. There they discovered three men with four casks. On being seen, the men threw down the casks and Gerhard took possession of them while Broadbridge ran to the beach. As the boat was now under sail again, he searched the most likely places for casks, but found nothing more.

A week later, on the night of 28 October, Broadbridge and Gerhard, aware that smugglers were active inland went together towards Colyford. They had two encounters with them but made no seizures until 2am when, on Axe Bridge, they saw a suspicious person coming towards them, It proved to be James Mill, a Beer smuggler. Suspecting therefore that smuggled goods were being brought that way, Gerhard kept Mill in his possession while Broadbridge ran towards Axmouth. He met the smugglers coming towards the bridge and seized fifteen casks of spirits. As Broadbridge states that he did not know either of the men, there were presumably only two, one of whom tried to run off with his two casks, dropping them only when Broadbridge called out and fired at him. Gerhard, leaving Mill, ran to assist Broadbridge, and the two officers remained on the spot until daylight, but discovered nothing more.

A few nights later, on 2 November 1815, Broadbridge and Gerhard working further west, seized three casks of foreign spirits in the parish of Salcombe from two men, one of whom was Robert Sparks of Seaton and Beer. The other man escaped. On the same night, in the parish of Sidbury, they seized one cask of brandy and two of geneva from Stephen Ham, again of Seaton and Beer.

Broadbridge and Gerhard's evidence seems to suggest that the casks/kegs/tubs were more likely to have been conveyed from the beach by men rather than by pack animals or carts. The most convenient way of doing this was in a harness over the shoulders, one tub at the front countered by the weight of the other at the back. The fact that some men carried only one tub suggests how heavy each must have been.

These, the recorded events of September, October and November 1815, give us quite a roll call of local smugglers. They were not necessarily part of Rattenbury's concern, for there was no shortage of smuggling entrepreneurs in Seaton and Beer in 1815 and 1816 to employ them, one of which was Daniel French.

On 2 April 1816, Broadbridge and Gerhard received information that the crew belonging to a boat owned by Daniel French had, at 9pm that night, put to sea at Seaton Hole for the purpose of taking up tubs and running them ashore. Taking with them Bernard McCandle and James Armstrong, two dragoons of the Inniskilling Regiment based at Seaton, the officers set off to intercept them. They separated, Broadbridge taking McCandle, and Gerhard taking Armstrong. It was a very dark night and, at about midnight, having reached Puttam's Yard on Seaton beach, Broadbridge noticed that warning fires were being lit about a hundred yards along the beach at the bottom at Sea Lane. He and McCandle ran to the place and found there three men, one of whom Broadbridge later claimed was Seaton mariner, Samuel Cox. All three men ran away and it was then, between the two fires, that Broadbridge saw Daniel French, whom he immediately accused of being concerned in making the fires. French denied it.

The first Daniel French to be recorded in the Seaton and Beer Parish registers was born in 1732. He married Mary Bishop in 1754. Their son, Daniel Bishop French, born in 1758, lived to be 76 years old and it is he who has the best 'form' as a smuggler, one sentence being served at Dorchester prison not long before his death in 1834. In 1777 he married Elizabeth, a member of the Wills family which also had smuggling connections. Their son Daniel was born soon afterwards. As Daniel French III was the same age as Rattenbury, it seems reasonable to assume that it was his father, Daniel Bishop French who owned the *Friends* in 1798, and who Broadbridge saw on Seaton beach in April 1816.

However, in 1815 and 1816, it was Rattenbury with his sloop *Volante*, who seems to have had the bigger smuggling boat, and he made full use of it:

> After one trip [in November 1815], I had been engaged to send six of the kegs of spirits to Lyme. As the three men were carrying them there, they were seized by the custom house officers who came to an agreement with the men to take them to their house [ie the Custom House at Lyme], but because one of the men ran away with some of the kegs, the other two men were detained in custody.

All three men were from Beer, The customs officer they encountered was Lyme tidewaiter Thomas Lock.

In the small hours of 14 November 1815, at Lyme, Lock met and seized from Thomas Westlake and John Small, four casks containing brandy and gin. He appears to have let the two men go only to encounter a third - Thomas Abbot - with another two casks, which he also seized. Unable to carry all six casks himself, he accepted Abbot's offer of help to carry them to the Custom House! Together they travelled about a quarter of a mile when Abbot, taking advantage of the fact that Lock was laden down with casks, absconded with his two. Lock pursued him. Abbot dropped one, but got away with the other.

This incident throws an interestingly light on the relationship between smugglers and customs officers at the time because Lock had been content to seize smuggled goods without necessarily detaining the smugglers. Had Abbot not abused Lock's trust, *none* of the three men would have been charged.

> The two men were to be brought to trial so, as I was absent at the time, my wife got bail for their appearance. I came home about a fortnight after and went to the trial. They were fined £25 each, beside expenses, which I and my partners paid for them, it being one concern. This was a very great loss, and severely felt by me.

Paying the fines of the men caught smuggling for them was a prudent course of action for any smuggling concern, for a man languishing in prison might be tempted to turn informer. Presumably it was William Dominy, and perhaps William Puttam, who shared the expense of the fines?

Soon after this event, several Sidmouth residents bought shares in the *Volante*. This was revealed when Charles Wild, the Sidmouth coastwaiter, reported the circumstances which in 1816 led him to seize the *Volante*'s oared boat. Rattenbury petitioned for its return, swearing it had not been involved in smuggling. He said that on 21 February he sent it to Sidmouth with its crew of four - William Loveridge, James Bartlett, Thomas Driver and John Bishop - to get a coil of rope for the *Volante*. Having got the rope, Rattenbury said they left Sidmouth the next day at 5pm, arriving back at Beer at 9pm, when two boatmen, George Mills and David Sterling, helped them to haul the boat ashore. Charles Wild, invited by the collector at Lyme to comment on Rattenbury's petition, was scornful.

> *"I beg leave to acquaint you that on 22 February last, the boat [of* Volante*] went from Sidmouth about 2 o'clock in the afternoon. That is the only word of truth that I can find in Raddenbury's petition. Instead of rowing away to the eastward for Beer, they rowed right off to the southward about three or four miles, and began to creep. In a short time they got hold of the raft [of tubs]. With my spyglass, I could see them haul up the goods and take them into the boat. This was the only smuggling boat that appeared upon this part of the coast that day, and in the evening they rowed along in west, which made me suspect that they would land at either Laderham [Ladram] or Windgates. I therefore stationed myself so as to watch both places. The goods were landed at Laderham a little after 6 o'clock in the evening, and carried up into a ploughed field in consequence of help not being come. As far as I have been able to learn, 35 kegs were landed.*
>
> *There are now at this place [Sidmouth] six new smugglers of Raddenbury's creation, they having a fourth part of the smuggling sloop* Volante *[presumably Dominy, Puttam and Rattenbury had the other three parts?] and they all agreed that if they had known I*

19. Clifton Row and High Peak from Sidmouth beach 1816

intended to seize the boat, I should have had some kegs instead. They would willingly have given me a pair each, as the Sloop cannot now go over [to France] for want of a boat.

On 16 March, on my return from the Customs House at Lyme, I called upon George Mills, Boatman at Beer. He informed me that he and David Sterling were on the beach at Beer when the Boat of **Volante** *came on shore there (which was at 9 o'clock on the evening of 22 February). He searched the boat very strictly, knowing that they had been out a-smuggling that day, but found nothing but a jar with about half a pint of brandy in, which he drank part of. There was no coil of rope in the boat. The only rope was that with which they had been creeping, and the mooring rope that the kegs had been sunk with, which was very wet, even although there was no rain that evening.*

Raddenbury has made a practice of keeping this boat at Sidmouth in order to go out and take up goods before Mr Curtis and the Boatmen at Beer can be aware of it, and she has never been employed in anything whatever except smuggling.

I humbly hope that their Honors will be pleased to observe that Raddenbury and his colleagues are most notorious smugglers belonging to Beer, and are always ready to swear to anything that will suit their smuggling purposes.

The kegs seized by me on the night of 22 February are marked with the initials of some of the owners of the Volante. *This boat [ie the oared boat belonging to the* Volante*] was built in Seaton two or three months ago entirely for smuggling and for no other purpose. She is a very complete Row Boat and will carry sixty or seventy kegs."* (PRO. Lyme Letterbooks CUST 63/1, 16 March 1816)

Wild then pointed out that it only took an hour to get from Sidmouth to Beer whereas, according to Rattenbury's reckoning, it had taken his men seven! Rattenbury did not get his row-boat back.

I made several other voyages to Cherbourg that summer [1816], all of which were successful, except one, where we lost half the cargo. After some winter voyages in the *Volante*, we laid her up to have her timbers fastened and to undergo general repair.

About this time a circumstance occurred which, though trivial in itself, occasioned me a great deal of vexation and trouble. About half a league from Beer, a smuggling boat was taken by the *Vigilant* cutter. It had only one man in it and, being acquainted with him, I and his brother, and four others, went on board to see if we could render him any assistance.

The captain was a good-natured man so I asked him to let the smuggler - his prisoner - come ashore with us. He refused, saying it was not in his power but, at parting, he gave us a bottle of gin. This was in my possession when we landed on the beach. The tidewaiter, who was measuring culm, asked me what I had got.

"A drop of gin," I said, whereupon he collared me and insisted on me giving it up. Determined to disappoint him, I threw it into the sea, so he wrote to the Board saying I had obstructed him in the performance of his duty. A short time afterwards, an order came from the board for my apprehension. He came to my house, attended by some soldiers, to take me up. I immediately surrendered myself, and they took me before the magistrates, who bound me over to appear at the ensuing Lammas assizes 1815, at Exeter. They set my bail at £200.

When the time arrived I went, employing attorney Kingdon and counsellor Moore to conduct my defence. The case was brought into court. The judge heard the evidence and, considering it frivolous and vexatious, honourably acquitted me.

It has not been possible to identify the Beer smuggler captured by the *Vigilant*, an Excise cutter stationed at Dartmouth, but the tidewaiter (or coastwaiter) who seized Rattenbury's gin might have been George Gerhard.

When the *Volante* had been repaired and was ready for sea, we made a few good voyages in her. On our return from the last, we left her lying in Lyme Cobb. A violent storm came on, and with the tide flowing at a great and unusual height she, along with several others, ran ashore and was dashed to pieces. With considerable difficulty, we succeeded in saving the materials.

The *Volante* foundered at Lyme on 20 January 1817.

CHAPTER 13

Beer Smugglers and Beer Boatmen
1816

The *Volante* was lost in January 1817, but she was smuggling throughout 1816 when the events related in this chapter took place.

Up to 1815, the Beer boatmen's watch house had been an old signal house at Beer Head. However, in September 1815, John Curtis learned that Lord Rolle, to whom the signal house belonged, had promised it to the Admiralty who wanted to 'erect telegraphs on the coast'. Curtis therefore suggested that a new watch house be erected on the same site as the shed which was then being built on Beer beach to house his crew's stores. The Board agreed. It cost them £71.

20. *An old preventive station*

John Curtis, like Charles Wild at Sidmouth, had a good understanding of smugglers and on 3 February 1816 supplied the Board with a report every bit as perceptive as that given by Wild about Rattenbury's activities in Sidmouth. It highlights the difficulties he,

110

his men, and local revenue cutter commanders, faced trying to prevent the trade.

"In answer to your letter of 31 January requesting my report on the present state of smuggling on this coast. It is now carried on to a pretty great extent, but solely in foreign spirits which are brought from Cherbourg in small casks which are moored in rafts from 6 to 12 miles from the shore. When it is impossible for us to launch off the beach, they [the smugglers] take them up in their large boats and land them in small quantities at a time, on different parts of the coast from Torbay to Portland. Notwithstanding our utmost vigilance, we can detect only a small proportion.

One way to prevent smuggling in this Bay [Lyme Bay] would be to establish one or two small craft of about 40 tons each (similar to the craft they smuggle in), commanded by men well versed in the nature of smuggling, and well acquainted with the coast. Such craft could lay on the coast with dead southerly winds, which are those the smugglers generally choose to come home on then, in a gale, they could make a harbour at Lyme Cobb, as the smugglers are often obliged to. The commanders of the large cutters are not fond of cruising in this deep bay when a strong onshore breeze is blowing. This is because they fear getting on shore, there being no harbour in the Bay for them to run too as there is insufficient water for vessels of their description at Lyme.

On Saturday last I had some idea that five different rafts were moored about seven or eight miles off Beer Head, and I communicated the same to the commanders of two revenue cruisers. I also informed them there were four large boats and a sloop [the Volante?] soon expected home. We swept the Sunday and Monday but without success. On Tuesday, a strong breeze to the south was blowing, so the cruisers got away under the west land for shelter. This morning, the boats and vessel arrived and moored their cargos, and seven large boats - taking advantage of the cruisers' absence, and knowing that there was too much surf to render it practicable for us [the boatmen] to come after them - launched and took up the rafts we were trying for. The cruisers were not able to return to the station from Torbay in time to prevent them from taking up the goods, but they did succeed in making the other boats moor again. However, they have moored under sail, and at such a distance from Beer, that it is now impossible for me to give the least idea where to sweep or creep. Had there been a small craft on the station of the description I have mentioned, it would have kept at sea longer, having Lyme to run for in case of emergency; then one or more of the craft that came home would have been detected.

I do not attach any blame whatever to the captains of the cruisers, as they have other objects in view, but I merely give it as my opinion that small craft are of greater utility in this bay to prevent smuggling than the large cutters, because you can disguise them to better deceive the smugglers, and they will keep the station longer." (PRO. Lyme Letterbooks CUST 63/1)

Severe weather conditions could prevent boatmen carrying out their duties. So could bribes. As Charles Wild indicated, bribes were a constant temptation, particularly in places like Beer and Sidmouth where the officers lived among the smugglers, and were in some cases related to them. Identifying a smuggler was not a difficulty for a revenue officer; it was apprehending him in circumstances likely to lead to a conviction that was problematic. And even this some officers may have been loathe to do if their neighbours were the friends and relations of the man they were going to send to prison.

Socially, the situation could not have been more complex, and that complexity worked against the effectiveness of the preventive effort. If, in time of need, a customs officer received more support from his smuggler neighbours than from his employers, then his loyalties were going to be divided, and his ability to do his duty compromised.

There is a suspicion that something of this nature occurred with Arthur Manning, who was for many years the riding officer at Chideock, another notorious smuggling blackspot. Between 28 January and 4 February 1816 he absented himself from duty and was ordered to attend at the Lyme Custom House to explain himself. Manning accepted that the charge was true but pleaded 'dire poverty', saying he was unable to maintain himself, his wife, and his family - he had five children - and was much in debt. No one accused him of directly aiding and abetting smugglers, but a man in such straightened circumstances was surely vulnerable to the financial overtures smugglers might make.

The problem is more starkly highlighted by the case of George Mills, the Beer boatman whom Charles Wild consulted in February 1816 about the *Volante's* boat. Two months later Mills was suspended from his post while the Board investigated a complaint by John Curtis that he had given information to the smugglers. He was 57 at the time and had been in the preventive service for forty years, first as a young crewman aboard revenue vessels and then, for 28 years, as a boatman resident in Beer. In 1813 his daughter Mary had married a local man called Leonard Prince.

Mills was eventually acquitted of the charge and allowed to return to his duties, but the suspicion lingered, breaking out into further accusations on 27 August 1816 when William Gibbs, a Beer fisherman, gave information against him at the Custom House in Lyme after the two men had quarrelled in a public-house. Mills had accused Gibbs of being the cause of his original suspension. Annoyed, Gibbs - despite James Orley pleading with him not to do so - went to the collector and told him that he had witnessed Mills decline to confiscate two jugs of spirits from smugglers Isaac Tidbury Snr and Isaac Tidbury Jnr, on Beer beach.

Over the next two months the case against Mills was examined, and among those called as witnesses were local men known to be smugglers. However, the first person the collector consulted was John Curtis. This is what Curtis wrote on 15 September 1816, just two weeks before his untimely death.

"In answer to your letter of 11 September respecting Mills, I have made every enquiry, but whether there exists any understanding between him and the smugglers, or not, I cannot positively say, as it is very difficult to procure any proofs in such cases, those with whom he may be connected finding it in their interest to keep it a profound secret. I can only say that circumstances that have come to my knowledge have rather confirmed a suspicion I have had for some time that he has not exactly acted the right and just part, and is a man that I cannot place confidence in as I would wish.

In the first place, one of our Boat's crew, being at Honiton, overheard some Beer smugglers say they supported Mills during the time he was suspended. William Gibbs - the complainant - also overheard Mills say to some smugglers, "Take care what you say to that man (meaning Gibbs), as he will acquaint the sitter with everything he knows"; and the generality of smugglers interesting themselves so much on his behalf - one [James Orley] offered to give any security to Gibbs for Mills' future behaviour to him provided he did not send his information to the Custom House - certainly has a suspicious appearance. Why would they interest themselves so much on his behalf unless they had some notion of being benefited by him, when I rather imagine they would rejoice to see the rest of the Boat's crew hung.

Whatever understanding - if any exists - between Mills and the smugglers is, in my opinion, carried on through the medium of his family at home, and through his daughter, who is married in this place to a man who smuggles pretty largely on his own account, and who also acts as an agent for others to sell their goods in the country.

Should the honourable Board think proper to shift him to another Boat so as to remove him from these connections, I think he would still make a good officer." (PRO. Lyme Letterbooks CUST 63/1)

Mills' son-in-law was Leonard Prince, and the two men Gibbs identified as smugglers were two Beer yeomen - William and George Mutter. They were the brothers of Abraham Mutter, who is reputed to have been a close smuggling associate of Rattenbury's.

Mills, speaking in his own defence on 16 October 1816, identifies another man as a smuggler:

> "I have no doubt that Gibbs comes forward from revenge in consequence of a public house quarrel between him and myself a few days before he made his complaint. He is a noted smuggler and would be glad to do me or my family any injury." (PRO. Lyme Letterbooks CUST 63/1)

What was the outcome of these many depositions? Mills does not appear to have been penalised. However, on 9 December 1816, John Peek, the new sitter, reported that Mills had served the preventive service with diligence and fidelity but was now afflicted by poor sight and rheumatism. It seems that he was retired on those grounds.

What complicated relationships smugglers and preventive men had with one another. And look how far they both ranged in pursuit of their activities. It seems unremarkable to them, if not to us, that they should have been drinking in the same Honiton pub!

Honiton, the birthplace of John Rattenbury's father, was on the main London to Exeter turnpike and it is therefore possible that the Beer smugglers had there some sort of 'safe' house where contraband was stored before onward transportation to markets arranged for them by someone like Leonard Prince.

By 1816, the government was well aware that the domestic situation of men like George Mills detracted from its anti-smuggling efforts therefore, in February 1816, as part of a rethink of the entire preventive strategy, boatmen started to be removed from their home neighbourhoods to stations further afield, where they would have fewer opportunities to collude with friends and relations. Cowes boatmen were sent to Swansea! Not surprisingly, the policy did not please the men and their families who, because of the unpopularity of customs officers, found it difficult to get accommodation in the places chosen for them. To overcome the problem, watch houses were built which incorporateed living quarters - the precursors of the coastguard cottages of the 1830s.

As part of the same re-organisation, most of the revenue cutters were transferred to the control of the Admiralty, leaving Customs with only two vessels and its riding officers. The waterguard was divided into 31 districts under the control of inspecting commanders, and then further divided into 140 stations, each station manned by a chief officer (or sitter), a senior boatman, and boatmen as before.

It was now the responsibility of the Admiralty to appoint cutter commanders, which they drew from a large reserve of naval lieutenants. Experienced in warfare not smuggling, the new breed of revenue commanders tended to resort rather too readily to firepower. The outbreak of peace had removed their opportunity to profit from captured foreign vessels. The only way they could enhance their naval salaries was by earning rewards for captured contraband and smugglers. This change of attitude increased the chances of violent confrontation with smugglers, who did not like being fired at at sea. Their response, on land at least, was to arm themselves with bludgeons and sticks and to go around in larger gangs. It was a most unfortunate development.

In the 1820s, Captain Frederick Marryatt (1792-1848) was one of those naval lieutenants. He commanded a revenue vessel on the south coast. In 1836 he published a novel called *The Three Cutters*, in which he describes a typical revenue vessel:

21. Cutter

"She is a cutter, and you may know she belongs to the Preventive Service by the number of gigs and galleys which she has hoisted up all round her. She looks like a vessel that was about to sail with a cargo of boats, two on deck, one astern, one on

the other side of her. You observe that she is painted black and much more lumbered up. Let us go on board; her bulwarks are painted red; it is not a very becoming colour, but then it lasts a long while, and the dockyard is not very generous on the score of paint, or lieutenants of the navy troubled with much spare cash.

She has plenty of men and fine men they are; all dressed in red flannel shirts and blue trousers; some of them have not taken off their canvas or tarpaulin petticoats, which are very useful to them, as they are in the boats night and day, and in all weathers. But we will at once go down to the cabin, where we shall find the lieutenant who commands her, a master's mate and a midshipman. They each have their tumbler in front of them and are drinking gin toddy, hot with sugar - capital gin too, above proof; it is from that small anker standing under the table. It is one that they forgot to return to the Custom House when they made their last seizure."

Marryat's description is valuable because between 1817 and 1821, Rattenbury had many encounters with revenue cutters and was sometimes called aboard them for interview with the captain or the mate. He never described the vessels in the detail that Marryat did.

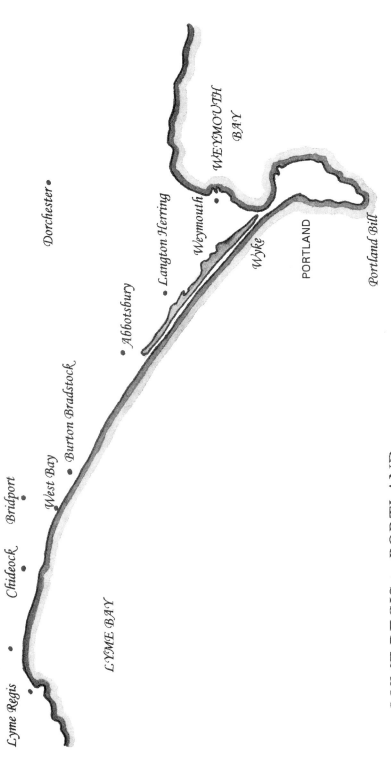

LYME REGIS to PORTLAND

CHAPTER 14

The *Elizabeth & Kitty*
1817

Soon after the loss of the *Volante*, Rattenbury salvaged and then purchased another sloop called the *Elizabeth & Kitty*. He describes this as happening in February 1816, but it was not until 1817 that his connection with the vessel began. Built at Brixham and registered at Dartmouth, the *Elizabeth & Kitty* was re-registered at Exeter on 16 May 1817 under the ownership of mariner James Good of Seaton and Beer, who was her master until 5 September when Abraham Sydenham took over.

It is interesting to note that, despite claiming to have been the owner, or part-owner of various vessels, Rattenbury's name should appear so infrequently in the local shipping registers. This was probably because he and his smuggling colleagues took it in turns to be the front man, or 'bondsman' for their co-operatively-owned vessels, so the registration document did not always reflect the true ownership of a boat, any more than it did the purpose for which it had been purchased. That the arrangement worked as well as it did indicates the level of trust between the group members. Sometimes the only way that customs officers could learn the true state of affairs was if one of the partners, or one of the boat's crew, was captured and turned informer; or if a disgruntled fellow smuggler (like William Gibbs perhaps?) offered information to the collector. But even in those circumstances, the information received could not necessarily be relied upon, and action was not always taken.

The following year, in February 1816 [1817], a fishing sloop called the *Elizabeth & Kitty*, belonging to Brixham, was driven into Beer roads in a gale of wind. When she came to an anchor, the crew left the vessel and took to the boat in which, at the imminent peril of their lives, they reached the shore.

I had an excellent row-boat so, with my son [probably William, 15] and two others, I went off to her. Once on board I found the water up to the cabin lockers. It had been my intention to carry her into Lyme, but we had no pump gear. The wind was blowing so hard that I was afraid she would not reach that port, so I ran her ashore on Seaton beach instead. For salvaging the vessel, I received remuneration, and afterwards agreed terms with the owners to purchase her. I managed to get the sloop into Axmouth harbour to be repaired. I then let her out for fishing, etc.

That summer [1817], I was seized with such a violent fit of sickness that my strength was much impaired, and I therefore made only two voyages during the course of it.

In September [1817], I went as a passenger in my own sloop, the *Elizabeth & Kitty,* to Cherbourg. There I hired a French vessel to bring a cargo home. It was a good voyage. I arrived safely and sent the French vessel back.

As preventive measures against smugglers became more effective, fewer escaped conviction, and fewer of their vessels escaped seizure. The loss of a boat could be a severe blow to a man whose family depended on it for their support. It might be seized for smuggling but without it a man could not go fishing either. As a precaution therefore, some smugglers sought alternative means of transporting contraband across the Channel and, like Rattenbury, used their own vessels to take them to France, and hired French vessels to bring them and their goods back.

In October [1817] I divided my sloop into shares and with my partners made seven voyages in her. On the first, we did very well. On the second, we got home and sunk the kegs, but the weather was so rough, they broke loose and drifted, and the officers took the greatest part of them. The third voyage was a short one and went well. Having some business to transact at home, I did not go on the fourth, but it turned out well. We saved nearly all of the fifth cargo, and the sixth proved a pretty good voyage too. The seventh and last was the best of all, for we landed all our goods, and disposed of them advantageously. We then laid up the vessel.

Abraham Sydenham of Beer, registered as the master of the *Elizabeth & Kitty,* was surely one of Rattenbury's partners? Was he, I wonder, the same Abraham Sydenham who on 7 October 1817, with William Gibbs of Beer - the same William Gibbs involved in the Mills case? - was petitioning the collector at Dartmouth for the return of their boat, the *Susan*, which had been seized in September 1817 by the *Vigilant* Excise cutter. At the time, the commander of the *Vigilant* was none other than Lt Daniel Miller, the man who had been in charge of the press gang at Teignmouth ten years earlier.

The knowledge of smuggling Miller had acquired in the Impress Service was invaluable to him in his new post, as Gibbs and Sydenham found to their cost. Both of them swore that the *Susan* had not been involved in smuggling, but Miller knew better.

"Abraham Sydenham is a notorious smuggler. Instead of fishing, she [ie the Susan] *was returning from Cherbourg, as I was informed by one of the crew called Abraham Summers. Sydenham*

119

informed me he had been only three days from Beer. On enquiry on shore, I [learned] from the officers of the Preventive Boat that they had been absent ten days."

Of the boat itself, Miller says she was:

"an Open Boat and, being foreign without licence, I seized her agreeable to law." (PRO. Dartmouth Letterbooks CUST 65/17)

In November, Sydenham and Gibbs were informed that they would not be getting their boat back because she had been operating beyond the limits of her licence, the argument customs officers increasingly used to counter the use of foreign registered vessels by smugglers. The two men were advised to apply for help to Lord Rolle, or to a Member of Parliament, if they wanted to carry the matter further.

22. *The* Vigilant *towing in the* Alfred *of London, December 1828*

Daniel Miller took over the command of the *Vigilant* in late 1816 or early 1817 and was with her for about two years. He made many seizures. One, in March 1817, was in conjunction with John Duffill, who had taken over from John Peek as sitter (now called the chief officer) of the Beer preventive boat. They captured the *Diane*, a Beer smuggling boat, with four men and 163 kegs aboard. In April, the *Glory* of Dartmouth was taken by the *Vigilant's* boat commanded by

Phillip Longworthy; and in October 1817, a sloop was taken with 113 casks. The four smugglers aboard were taken before the magistrates, probably in Dartmouth where the *Vigilant* was based. One, a Frenchman, was discharged, but the other three were fined £25 each. One paid and was liberated but the other two had no funds and were committed to Devon County Gaol in Exeter.

The activities of Beer smugglers' accomplices on land were also recorded. In June 1817, boatman Daniel Richards spotted Nicholas Driver of Beer watching the movements of his colleagues, then saw him light warning fires. A few days later Richards detected another two men doing the same thing in a field called Milk Pier, situated at the back of Beer. They were farmer James Thomas, and inn-keeper Samuel Hammett, the same man who, in 1814, was registered as a vintner. Both were described by John Duffill as being 'in the habit of dealing very largely in smuggled spirits'.

At 3am on 1 July, Richards and fellow boatman Sam Freeman were in Mare Lane, Beer when, on a hill called South Down, they discovered a man with a tub on his back. He was later identified as Jacob Phillips, a local man.

At about 11pm on the night of 7 July, John Hook, the 15-year-old son of a Beer boat builder, was on Beer cliff signalling to smugglers at sea with a lantern. He was detected by John Duffill. 'The smugglers are now in the habit of employing children to make their signals, as they think their age will be a protection for them,' said Duffill. It did not protect young John Hook who, along with Nicholas Driver, was committed to gaol for non-payment of the fines imposed upon them by magistrates.

Also in July 1817, Seaton fisherman and smuggler, Samuel Cox, was caught at sea with four other men and taken into Portsmouth. Three of the men 'consented' to be seamen but Cox, being disabled in one arm, was imprisoned instead.

The riding officers were active too. On 18 August, Richard Broadbridge reported that he searched the cart of a man called Harris, a 'great smuggler' who kept the horse and cart mainly for carrying contraband. However, Broadbridge found nothing in the cart except an empty box bearing the name of G Coppleston of Exeter. Coppleston wrote to the collector at Exeter complaining in the strongest terms that his property had been unjustly apprehended by Broadbridge.

Although John Rattenbury and his colleagues were smugglers, it should not be forgotten that had they been able to obtain a decent living by more regular pursuits, most would probably have done so. Smuggling was not an easy option. Imprisonment and impressment could leave their families just as poorly provided for unemployment due to the loss of a boat. In 1819 four Beer seamen - Henry Hetchley 45, Joseph Miller 36, Thomas Newton 32, and Henry Newton 23, were impressed aboard HMS *Queen Charlotte*.

Drowning was another occupational hazard. Smugglers usually operated in winter, and in weather conditions which would keep revenue cutters in harbour and revenue boatmen on the shore, so they took risks. Sometimes the risks paid off, but there were occasions when a smuggler paid with his life. Bearing testimony, the Seaton and Beer parish register covering the years 1816-1825 includes a roll-call of local men reported to have been drowned whilst smuggling. The toll in 1816 was five - James Akuman, Richard Stokes, Philip Gaverick, Robert Seller, and James Whitemore.

The sea was not fussy who it claimed and on 13 June 1817, a galley from HMS *Queen Charlotte* - the very ship on which Henry Hetchley and his companions were later impressed - was lost in a gale off Sidmouth while cruising for the prevention of smuggling. Eight seaman, all described as volunteers, perished. In December 1819, five sailors attached to the Weymouth revenue cutter *Greyhound* drowned while carrying out their duties.

In 1817, unusually for Rattenbury, he was using his sloop *Elizabeth & Kitty* for legitimate trading purposes:

> In April 1817, in an open boat with three other men, I crossed to Cherbourg, making two safe voyages in succession. In July of the same year, in the *Elizabeth & Kitty*, I went to Southampton with a cargo of stones and coal. Having discharged it, we took in a load of slate, and the vessel went to sea. Having some business of importance to transact, I stayed behind. As soon as it was finished, I set off for home by coach. When I arrived, I had the satisfaction of learning that the vessel had already discharged her cargo.
>
> In October, one of my partners and myself went as passengers to Cherbourg, where we again hired a French vessel to take in a cargo of contraband goods, with which we returned. All went well. We then made several other voyages there and back, sometimes safe, sometimes partly so.
>
> In the meantime, the *Elizabeth & Kitty* was captured by the *Vigilant* cutter. All her goods and one man were taken. He, on being promised his liberty and £20, turned informer, and disclosed all particulars as to whom the goods belonged. The vessel was then taken into Dartmouth and forfeited to the Government.
>
> In conjunction with two others, I then bought a small French vessel, in which we made several good voyages, carrying on a prosperous trade till the close of the year, which helped to repair the loss we had sustained.

Rattenbury's 'we' indicates that those involved with him in smuggling in his French vessel were the same men who had been his partners in the *Elizabeth & Kitty*. If so, then one of them was surely the master, 'notorious smuggler' Abraham Sydenham, so did Rattenbury have something to do with Sydenham and Gibbs' French vessel the *Susan*, also captured by Miller?

East Devon smugglers purchased and registered vessels in France in order to protect them from confiscation if they were caught ferrying contraband but, as we have seen, this did not always work. They therefore also hired French vessels owned by Frenchmen, which the customs officers did not find so easy to impound.

> In January 1817, a vessel that had been to Sidmouth with coal was drive into Loden Bay in a violent storm. She was obliged to let go her anchor and cut away her cable, and so ran ashore at Seaton beach. Being a fine vessel, well adapted for coasting, myself and a friend purchased her of the owner, a Mr Flinn [William Flinn the younger, of Exmouth?]. She was so much damaged that it was with considerable difficulty that we got her into Axmouth harbour. There we had her properly repaired. In June she was ready for sea and my partner, together with my son [William, 15], took the first voyage in her. They went to Newquay for a cargo of slate.
>
> In the meantime, with some other smugglers, I had a long open boat built in France. In July, when she was finished, I went over to Cherbourg. Having taken in a cargo of goods, I employed Frenchmen to assist me in bringing her home. We put to sea, but less than two hours later two long-boats belonging to the custom house gave chase. Altering our course, we succeeded in getting back again.
>
> On the following morning, which was a Wednesday, we sailed again, but about 4 o'clock in the afternoon, before we realised she was there, another long-boat came alongside of us. She chased us for about three hours. We were boarded but they found nothing because we had thrown our kegs out. Nevertheless we were taken into Alderney and put on board the *Adder*.

The *Adder* ketch, though attached to Dartmouth, was based in Alderney. Her captain was Richard Bowden.

> The captain examined us. Finding that it was a French boat manned by French sailors, and that I was rated a passenger, he told us to go about our business, but added: "I have a great mind to keep you in consequence of your having given me so much trouble. Be sure that if ever I come across you again, you throw out your tubs fairly, that I may take them up". To this proposition I agreed, not wanting any obstacles in the way of regaining my liberty.
>
> On Friday, about 12 o'clock, we sailed from Alderney for Cherbourg, where we arrived at about half-past three. We stayed there that night and on Saturday morning took in another lot of goods. On Sunday, we set sail. On Monday, we arrived home and sunk our goods. The Frenchmen put me on shore at Lyme and took the long-boat back to

France. We had a great deal of difficulty taking up our kegs, and lost a considerable part of them.

By this time, our vessel [the one purchased from Flinn] had arrived from Newquay with her cargo of slate. She then took in a load of culm, with which she proceeded to Charmouth. There she landed, but a gale prevented the crew from getting to sea again. Although she had an anchor out, the cable parted and she drifted ashore and went to pieces.

I received a letter from my partner and my son giving an account of their misfortunes, and asking me to come. I accordingly took a horse, and went to them as fast as possible.

23. Charmouth beach

We succeeded in saving the sails and the greatest part of the materials, which we carried into Lyme and deposited in a sail loft. When they had been put in order, an estimate was taken of them, and I bought my partner's half for the trifling sum of £13. Our loss had been great because the vessel had cost about £200, and she had only made her second voyage.

In August [1817], a French vessel in which I had a share came to Lyme, and together with another smuggler, I went over to Cherbourg in her. The speculation turned out profitably.

One of my creditors at this time - the brewer to whom I was in debt for £100 when I gave up the public house - heard that I had purchased the wreck at Lyme and took out a writ against me. I went to his house and agreed to give him £25 in hand and £25 later. Having paid these sums he gave me a full discharge so that I was once more clear of the world, which was a great satisfaction to my mind.

I then went smuggling again, and made several voyages, some of which were profitable. Others proved unsuccessful.

In the latter part of the year, a strong wind drove a Swedish schooner into the bay. Being on the look-out, I saw her and immediately went on board. I agreed with the captain to take him into Lyme for £40. The vessel was in such a leaky state however that I was obliged, with their assistance, to use every exertion to save her. At last we got her in safe, which pleased the captain, who paid the money ungrudgingly.

CHAPTER 15

Encounters with Revenue Cutters from Dartmouth and Weymouth 1818-1820

At the beginning of 1818, John Rattenbury was 39 years old and the father of five children - William 16, Frances Nichols 12, John Partridge 8, Ann 5, and Abraham Henry 1.

> In January 1818, I was laid up by a severe fit of the gout, which continued for two months and proved a considerable hindrance to me in business. It threw me greatly back in the world for I had a large family.
>
> When I recovered and could get about again I started fishing and smuggling and in those activities I was employed for the remainder of the year, and for the spring of the next. I was pretty successful.

1818 may have been a quiet year for Rattenbury, but it was not a quiet year for Daniel Miller aboard the *Vigilant*, or for the crew of the *Scourge* revenue cutter which, under its new commander Lt Robert McCrea, arrived at its new base of Lyme early in 1818. With it came John Peek, John Duffill's predecessor as chief officer of the Beer boat. He had gone to Dartmouth to live but now reappeared as a crewman on the *Scourge*.

On 16 May 1818 the *Scourge*, in conjunction with the *Greyhound* cutter of Weymouth commanded by Lt Nugent, fished up off Abbotsbury in Dorset a raft of tub which gave rise to a typical dispute between the two commanders over the reward, with McCrea complaining bitterly that Nugent's report made his look false.

On 11 July, the *Scourge* was in action again, chasing for six hours a smuggling lugger which McCrea described as an open boat, painted white, with rigged weather cloth, six oars muffled, and with sweep and mark lines - all the accoutrements required for smuggling. During the last hour of the chase, the *Scourge* got into the lugger's wake and those aboard her, unable to escape, sunk their tubs and ran the vessel ashore on a small bay to the east of Strait Point. Three crewmen, dressed like English sailors and with packages on their backs, jumped out of the boat under the musket fire of the *Scourge*'s crew, and escaped across the field. McCrea's men took possession of the vessel, which proved to be the *Cygne* fishing boat of Cherbourg whose dimensions exceeded those described in the registry document. In her were four Frenchman who said they had been fishing, but there were no fishing nets in the boat. The Frenchmen said they had put the nets down in the Channel but McCrea was sure it was tubs they had put down, but the weather had been so thick at the time of the chase, he did not know where.

It was canny move on the part of the smugglers to hire French vessels to convey contraband, as the outcome of the seizure at Beer of the *Quatre Frères* (*Four Brothers*) of Cherbourg demonstrates:

On 24 May 1818 John Duffill and George Gerhard, now a riding officer, detained a 12-ton sloop called the *Quatre Frères*, which was owned by August Maurice Poupard of Cherbourg, where it had been registered two months earlier on 28 March. At the same time, they seized the *Five Brothers* - a Beer boat owned by William Gibbs - for landing spars and masts taken from the *Quatre Frères*

In their separate petitions to the Board, Poupard and Gibbs claimed that the spars were wreck goods found in the Channel by the *Quatre Frères* and given to Gibbs when he came out from Beer to inquire if she needed a pilot.

Poupard's petition came through a French consul; Gibbs' was supported by Seaton and Beer churchwardens, Roger Chown and William Brown. They said Gibbs, who had a large family, was an industrious man 'totally unconnected with smuggling'. If this is the same William Gibbs already referred to in this book, then that statement must have been greeted with hoots of derision at the Custom House!

The churchwarden's reference to smuggling is apt because that is what the seizure of the two vessels was really about. Duffill was sure that Poupard - who admitted in his petition to earning a living by hiring out his vessel for fishing and passenger carriage, sometimes between France and England - had just returned from a trip organised by Beer smugglers. Having sunk the tubs, Poupard was returning his passengers - one of whom would have taken bearings at the place the goods were sunk - and William Gibbs had gone out to him to take them off.

Duffill believed that four notorious Beer smugglers were involved with the *Quatre Frères* and that, during the winter, she had been constantly employed bringing tubs of spirits from Cherbourg. He also believed that the four smugglers had purchased a boat for William Gibbs after Gibbs had threatened 'to swear against her and another vessel belonging to Beer'. Duffill did not, in this instance, name the four smugglers, but one could well have been John Rattenbury. If not then it is further evidence that just about anybody in Beer with access to a boat, was involved in smuggling in some way.

Gibbs did not get his boat back, but Poupard did. Reluctant to confiscate a French-owned vessel, the Board ordered Poupard's sloop be delivered up to him.

Daniel Miller was thwarted in a similar way. On 15 February 1818, he seized, on suspicion of an intent to smuggle, a Roscoff lugger called *Theodore*. Aboard her were two Englishman, one American, and eight Frenchmen. No contraband was found but Miller was convinced that she had sunk her cargo before capture. The French consulate again protested and, unable to find the sunken raft of kegs which would have proved his case, Miller reluctantly released the *Theodore* into the charge of her crew.

It was unusual for Miller not to get his way, for he was as diligent in seizing smuggling vessels as he was in claiming the rewards from the Board afterwards:

> *"There being condemned in the last term, as prizes to HM Revenue Cruiser under my command,* St Joseph *French lugger and her boat, the* Pilewell *cutter and her boat, and a lugsail boat called* Susan *of Beer, and the reward for the spirits seized have been duly paid for. [However] I have to request you will oblige me by moving the Honble Commissioners of Customs to give orders that the above vessels may be disposed of according to law. Although every care possible is taken of them by the officers of the Customs at this port, by laying up so long they receive damage, which reduces their value. Daniel Miller, Lt and Commander."*
> (PRO. Dartmouth Letterbooks CUST 65/18, 23 February 1818)

Rattenbury's vessels had to run the gauntlet of many revenue cruisers, but in 1819 it was the *Adder* and her Captain, Richard Bowden, he had most to fear from.

> In June 1819, together with another smuggler, I went to Cherbourg. Having taken in a cargo, we put to sea in the long-boat of which I have spoken before. When off Start Point, we fell in with the *Sea Gull* tender belonging to the *Adder* sloop-of-war [the *Adder* revenue ketch].
>
> The sea was calm so we perceived her a long way off and therefore got alongside a large Dutch ship in the hope that it would conceal us from them. There we remained for some time, but at last the crew on board the tender spied us, hove out their boat, and gave chase.
>
> We spread all the canvass we could to try to make our escape, but we had no wind, and the four Frenchmen on board were indifferent sailors. The tender's boat was a fine one, and well manned, so they at last came up with us. However, they could not find a single article on board to confirm their suspicion of our being smugglers, nor had they seen us throw anything out.
>
> While they were deliberating, the sitter of the boat recollected my physiognomy, and remembered that I had promised his captain that, if they fell in with me again, I would throw my kegs over fairly, that he

might pick them up. It was on that condition I had suffered no injury. So the sitter took me on board the tender.

As soon as the commander saw me, he exclaimed: "You're a pretty fellow to throw your things out in such a manner after promising so fair! And after the leniency I showed towards you!" He then said that there was a new act respecting smugglers, and that he was going to take us into Dartmouth.

24. Dartmouth Custom House (on the right), at Bayard's Cove

When we arrived there, he took us to the Custom House to be examined by the collector. The collector had not arrived at the office and I seized an opportunity to make my escape in a small boat across the water to King's Wear [Kingswear]. From thence I got to Brixham.

The same afternoon, I received a letter from a landlord at Dartmouth, informing me that the case had been investigated at the Custom House and nothing found against me. As he requested me to come over about the Frenchmen's bill, I went to his house the following Sunday, but had scarcely sat down when I was surrounded by the men belonging to the tender by whom I was first taken. They insisted on my going with them as their prisoner. Greatly aggravated by this treachery, I refused, and prepared to make a staunch resistance, so they sent a man away to fetch two constables.

Upon hearing the case the constables said that as it was Sunday and they did not have a warrant from the magistrates, they would not interfere. Realising how resolute I was, the men belonging to the tender asked if I would give them my passport and appear on the morrow. I agreed, they departed, and I returned home.

About three weeks later an order came down from the Board for the boat to be delivered up, but by sending her back to France I and my companions got out of yet another difficulty.

The Custom House in Dartmouth is at Bayard's Cove, a picturesque quay featured to such good effect in the television series *The Onedin Line*.

25. Bayard's Cove, Dartmouth

Rattenbury appears to have been the organiser and paymaster of his smuggling concern. The French crew of his long-boat had either stayed in lodgings in Dartmouth before the trip or, having been released by the magistrates, had stayed there afterwards for it was their bill he was called upon by their landlord to pay. The landlord's subsequent treachery is an indication of how keen customs officers at Dartmouth were to catch Rattenbury, which is why he switched his activities to the Weymouth area. However, his troubles with the men of the *Sea Gull* tender, and the *Adder* cutter, were not yet over:

> Soon after this business was settled, I and one of my companions went as passengers in a boat to France. Off Portland, we again fell in with the boat belonging to the same cutter. Having a complaint in my eyes, my face was muffled up so the sitter did not recognise me.
>
> "What's the matter with that old fellow?" they asked my companions, to which some indifferent answer was given.
>
> By this time, the cutter had come up and was within hailing distance. The commander ordered his people to bring to him the person who had the command of the boat, which they did. He was examined, and asked several questions, one of which was, what had become of me?
>
> "When you see him," said the commander [Bowden], "tell Rattenbury that if ever I fall in with him again, I will hang him up at the yard-arm. He destroys all." He then sent our captain about his business. The fact that they had not recognised me afforded no small merriment to us all!
>
> Having got rid of the cutter, we proceeded to Cherbourg where we hired a vessel. We stayed there two or three days, taking in our cargo, after which we put to sea again, and got home safe and well.

On land in 1819, Richard Broadbridge, sometimes assisted by Beer boatmen, made several seizures. In January, watching at Culverhole after having seen men go out from Seaton beach to a vessel offshore, he foiled a landing and captured three casks of brandy and four of geneva. One of the men carrying the casks was William Gibbs, and on 12 March Broadbridge went to Beer to arrest him; but Gibbs had absconded. Broadbridge did manage to seize the boat. It was the *Fortuna* of Beer, which was not licensed.

On 11 May, again on Seaton beach, he saw a suspicious boat hovering at sea, but a fire at Seaton Hole warned it off. As he had seen two smugglers cross the River Axe, he made a signal with his handkerchief to alarm the men in the Beer boat, which had gone into Axmouth. With the help of boatmen Thomas King and William Simcs he secured 28 tubs of brandy, while William Hames seized the boat and its crew, who were Henry Partridge, William Newton, and Thomas Westlake. All three were taken before the Sidmouth magistrate, who sent them to prison in Exeter. To Broadbridge's dismay, they were given bail and were soon back on his patch.

A new feature in the entries in customs letterbooks for this period is the number of claims made by Broadbridge, Gerhard and Duffill, for a share of the fines paid by the smugglers they had apprehended. On 1 April, Duffill claimed a share, for himself and his boat's crew, of the

£50 paid at the previous Exeter assizes by Samuel Hammett and James Thomas for making a warning fire.

It has not been possible to discover whether any of the men mentioned in these reports was arrested as a result of being involved in Rattenbury's activities, but a Thomas Westlake crewed and carried tubs for him in November 1815.

In 1819, Rattenbury and his partners saw an opportunity to get back their sloop *Elizabeth & Kitty*. They took it:

> In September the same year [1819] my partner went to Dartmouth and repurchased the *Elizabeth & Kitty*, the vessel we had lost.

It was a little earlier. The *Elizabeth & Kitty* was registered at Lyme on 13 February 1819 when she was described as a square-sterned smack of nearly 25 tons, with one deck and one mast. Her owner was Lyme mariner William Saunders, who was her master until 4 November 1819 when William Horsford took over.

> In October we got her ready for sea and made a voyage in her to Cherbourg, where we took in a cargo of goods, which we brought home and landed safely.
>
> Our second voyage was to the same place and proved just as successful. However, on the third voyage, while we were about a league off shore between Lyme and Seaton, we spied a sail. Being suspicious, we hauled our wind and went about to the eastward. Being in the moon of the vessel, they could see our motions, but we could not see theirs. We kept away to the westward. About half an hour later, we saw it was a cutter and that she was in pursuit of us.
>
> Before long she came up and fired several musket shots at us. We hauled our boat up. I told everyone to get into it as quick as possible, and to hold her on. I then laid down the helm, and jumped in with them. The cutter had to luff [head into the wind] to avoid running on board our vessel. We made our escape, but we left behind 300 kegs of spirits and several bales of tea.
>
> We spread all the sail we could and, afraid to land at Beer in case the crew of the cutter were in pursuit of us, we came ashore about a mile and a half away. We made our way home, leaving our boat behind.
>
> A few days later I heard that the cutter's captain was at Lyme so I sent my wife to him to ask if he would be kind enough to deliver up the clothes we had left on board. He told her that, if I came for them myself, I could have them.
>
> I went to him and he received me very civilly being, I suppose, in a good temper at having taken so fine a prize. In the course of our interview, he showed me a pocket-book which he had found.
>
> "Is it yours?" he asked.
>
> "No," I replied, "but I know who it belongs to. If you will have the goodness to entrust it to me, I will deliver it to the owner."

He then gave me the pocket-book, and all the clothes, and I returned home. I was depressed at the loss I had sustained but consoled myself with the thought that it might have been worse, for I was still in possession of my liberty. This happened in November 1819.

This incident happened not in November 1819 but at 10pm on Saturday 18 November 1820, and it was not a cutter which chased the *Elizabeth & Kitty*, but a boat belonging one, in this case the *Greyhound* of Weymouth, commanded by Lt Anderson. It was therefore Lt Anderson with whom Rattenbury had the interview.

Richard Buck, one of the *Greyhound*'s mariners, had been in charge of the boat, and two days later he filed this report:

"While cruising off Portland on Saturday night last, at about 10 o'clock we fell in with a suspicious looking sloop to which I immediately gave chase, during which she threw over a number of casks. She cut away her boat from her stern while the bowman of my boat had hold of her and was in the act of hauling her up alongside.

I directly put two of my men into the sloop boat to look for the casks, continuing the chase myself when about midnight the sloop ran on shore near Langton [Langton Herring] and has gone to pieces, I being unable to land.

In returning to look for the casks during Sunday, I fell in with Mr Gover, who had launched from the beach and had secured forty casks of spirits and three casks of tea." (PRO. Weymouth Letterbooks CUST 59/36)

John Gover was in command of another of the *Greyhound*'s boats. He and his crew had been sent in search of the tubs thrown overboard from the *Elizabeth & Kitty*. They found them, but not in the sea. They were aboard a Portland fishing boat belonging to Robert White. White handed the casks over to Gover and his crew, but wrote to the Board claiming salvage. This was White's deposition:

"On 19th November, at 6 o'clock in the morning, having been informed that during the night a vessel had been wrecked on the beach at Abbotsbury, [Robert White] went in his boat with four men from Portland to render assistance. On returning from the wreck (which proved to be the sloop Elizabeth & Kitty *of Lyme), a distance of eight miles, about 3 o'clock in the afternoon, off Wyke, they fell in with thirty casks of spirits and three casks of tea floating in the water. These they took into the boat and immediately made a signal to the officers in the* Greyhound *boat, then off Wyke, to come to take charge of them. Mr Gover, the deputed officer, rowed alongside and came into [Robert White's]*

boat. Shortly afterwards, they picked up six more floating casks of spirits, the whole of which was delivered to the charge of the said Mr Gover and landed on the beach at Wyke. [Robert White] now craves that your Honors will be pleased to direct that what salvage the law allows shall be paid to him and his boat's crew for picking up these 36 casks of spirits and three casks of tea." (PRO. Weymouth Letterbooks CUST 59/36)

Lt Anderson was unimpressed by this account. He said that when the crew of the *Greyhound*'s boat encountered White's boat, they:

"observed one of the men in her stand up and wave. When alongside, John Gover found that the people in her had picked up a great number of casks which were, of course, given up by them. However, Gover is confident from the character and occupations of the individuals that they would never have done so had he not been pulling towards them and too near to prevent a possibility of their getting away unseen. Also it was evident that they were afloat for the express purpose of looking for these casks. Had they been returning - as they state - from the wreck, there was no need to cruise about, as they could have fetched back with the wind as it then was. Under these circumstances, and knowing these men to be smugglers, I refused to give them anything for their trouble. H Anderson." (PRO. Weymouth Letterbooks CUST 59/36)

What is interesting about these reports is the connection they suggest between the *Elizabeth & Kitty* and known smugglers from Portland. Anderson believed that Robert White knew the location of the *Elizabeth & Kitty*'s tubs. Had White been involved in the smuggling operation? Had he been employed by the smugglers to retrieve the lost tubs?

In his informative book *Dorset Smugglers*, Roger Guttridge published a list of smugglers, categorised by parish, which he derived from research in prison records. Even at a glance, it is obvious that the most extensive entries for Dorset are for Portland, and the most extensive entries for Devon are for Beer. Off the coast of Abbotsbury on November 1820, we now know there was a smuggling incident which involved *both* of those smuggling fraternities.

In Guttridge's list, the name White features no less than eleven times in a twenty-year year period, mostly belonging to fishermen, and several to fisher*women*! Women *did* smuggle. In the same month Rattenbury lost his sloop, the Weymouth Harbour preventive boat seized a large amount of contraband liquor from women. The fact that it was being carried not in casks but in bladders suggests that it may have been concealed beneath their skirts. Between the 4th and 24th

November, no less than 29 bladders were seized from ten women and girls on eight separate occasions.

Rattenbury was soon smuggling again, although the events he describes next may well have preceded the loss of the *Elizabeth & Kitty*.

In the latter end of December [1819?], I went over to Cherbourg again, in a vessel as a passenger with another man. Having taken in our cargo, we set sail on 2 January 1820 [1821?], and arrived the next morning off the English coast.

The sea was calm so we took our goods in the boat intending to land them. Within three quarters of an hour of leaving the vessel, a tremendous gale came on, accompanied by heavy snow, which half filled the boat. The air was so intensely cold that we were almost frozen, but in this situation we had to remain until morning because the atmosphere was so dense we could not see the vessel, and those on board her could not see us.

About 7 o'clock, having spied the signal we had hoisted, those on the vessel came alongside and took us on board. We shifted our clothes, all of us half dead with the sufferings we had endured. We sunk our kegs and went on shore, but because of the violence of the gale, some of the kegs drifted and were lost.

About the same time, the little French vessel of which I had purchased half, came out of Cherbourg and fell in with the *Hind* sloop of war. She was captured with all her cargo. As may be imagined, this crushed my hopes and threw a fresh gloom over my spirits. When the mind has been long trained in adversity it becomes callous to disappointments. Though its ardour may be for a while repressed, its powers of endurance are not easily subdued.

CHAPTER 16

A Marked Man
1820-1821

In February 1820 we find Lt McCrea of the *Scourge* cutter, disputing a seizure not with the commander of another revenue vessel, but with John Duffill and his Beer boatmen. It arose as a consequence of two preventive boats being operated out of Beer: the regular boat, and another owned by extraman Sam Stagg and manned by a crew from the *Scourge*. The subject of the dispute was the sunken cargo of the *Brothers* of Beer, consisting of 126 tubs, crept up between Salcombe Mouth and Weston by the *Scourge*. The Beer boatmen claimed it was they who had located it. In the same month, Rattenbury was off to Cherbourg for a cargo of tubs:

> In February 1820, with three other passengers, I went to Cherbourg, where we hired a French vessel. Having taken in our cargo, we got home with the loss of part of it, then sent the vessel back. About this period I was laid up with a severe attack of the gout. After six weeks, the disorder relaxed its grasp and I was able to walk about again.

Rattenbury makes no mention of the fact that on 18 March 1820, his son William 18, Robert Woodgate 23, Richard Hooper 23, Thomas Westley 43, and thirty-four casks, were captured just off Weymouth aboard the *Mary* of Beer by the *Greyhound* cutter commanded by Lt Anderson. All four men, described as fishermen, were convicted of smuggling and sent to Dorchester prison, from which they promptly escaped! Only William Rattenbury was recaptured, and on 9 December 1820, Lt Anderson, who had received a reward of £20 for his capture the first time, claimed another for his recapture, even though William had already been liberated by court order.

The prison records give a full description of John Rattenbury's eldest son. He was of middle height, with very dark brown hair, a dark complexion, dark hazel eyes, and two pock marks between his eyebrows. There were two slight cuts over the left eyebrow. The eyes of his three fellow-smugglers are described as being grey, or dark grey. Henry Hetchley, Joseph Miller, and Thomas and Henry Newton, held at Dorchester the same year, had similar colouring.

One interesting theory put forward to explain why the complexions of the inhabitants of Beer were so swarthy was that they were of Spanish extraction. In 1871, Francis Kilvert suggested that either a ship of the Spanish Armada was wrecked at Beer in 1588, or that in about 1700, a Spanish ship went ashore nearby. In both cases the result was a colony of Spaniards who intermarried with the local inhabitants. There is no evidence to support these notions. The inter-marrying of families would have been sufficient to ensure a likeness between individuals in whom the genetic pool was already biased towards men and women of short to middle height with dark hair and grey eyes. There is no indication that John Rattenbury differed markedly in appearance from other Beer residents.

In May [1820], I was on the beach at Beer when a gentleman landed. I fell into conversation with him. Learning that he had come into the neighbourhood in order to take excursions by sea during the summer, I offered my services. Unable to find a vessel he liked, he bought one that I had and converted it into a pleasure yacht, and when he went to sea in it, he employed my son [William?] constantly, and myself occasionally.

I accompanied him to Sidmouth, Dartmouth, Brixham, and other places on the western coast and, as the summer advanced, to Guernsey and Jersey with a party of his friends.

At Jersey I fell extremely ill, and I will never forget the kindness and humanity with which the gentleman provided medical assistance for me. He supplied my various wants till I recovered, then we resumed our expedition. After having seen what was remarkable in the Channel Islands, we turned back, arriving at Seaton where we put the ladies and gentlemen on shore. They were delighted with their tour, and with the many interesting scenes and curious objects they had examined in the course of it. I felt no less grateful for the kindness which they had shown me, and for the liberal manner in which they promised to reward my services and attendance. In this, however, I was sadly disappointed.

That summer I bought a small spot of ground with a view to building a house, and went with my boat along the cliffs, picking up stones to erect it with. Throughout the fall I was busily employed getting all the materials ready for the carpenters and masons to begin work.

Then in September, with some friends, I went to sea to take up some kegs which we had sunk. It being night, a preventive boat came close before we saw it. One of the men in it laid hold of the outrigger, but I jerked his hand off and put our boat out of their grasp. Having no sail they were obliged to take to their oars to chase us. They fired at us. A fine breeze sprang up so the longer they pursued us, the more we left them astern. Finding their efforts useless, they gave up the case, and we got safe on shore.

During what remained of the fair weather that year I helped with my house, and attended the gentlemen whenever he went to sea, or required my services.

In November, a boat of mine came home and, having sunk her goods, was driven on shore. Soon after this misfortune another took place when a boat of mine was stranded on Stapen sands [Slapton Sands?]. She was dashed to pieces, and the greater part of the goods became the prey of the inhabitants.

In the same month I went to Weymouth, and took all the money I could collect, and paid my merchants.

In 1820 Rattenbury's smuggling activities were undoubtedly centred around Weymouth, as the wrecking of the *Elizabeth & Kitty* near Abbotsbury, and the involvement of Robert White of Portland in the retrieval of some of her casks, indicates. Who was it, I wonder, Rattenbury was collecting money from?

26. *The quay at Weymouth*

While I was in Weymouth, the Lyme packet bound for Guernsey with passengers, was driven in during a gale. On Saturday, the day on which she had appointed to set sail, the captain got drunk so the passengers left him. On Sunday he put to sea, and myself and one of my partners, went with him to Cherbourg where we took on board a cargo, with which we returned. We were passengers on the same vessel.

After about fourteen hours we came to Salcombe hill [near Sidmouth] and hove the boat out. Myself and a boy who was with us, got into her to try to get on shore, but the surf was so great near the beach, it was impossible to land. We went off again intending to return to the vessel, but the weather was so hazy we could not find her. We then tried to land again. The first sea we saved, but seeing there was great danger from the second, I jumped overboard and swam to the shore. Looking around, I had the satisfaction of discovering that the boy had also escaped. The boat had capsized.

We went to Sidmouth as quickly as possible. There we found ashore some of the men belonging to the packet, so we sent them after the boat.

At dawn the next morning we saw the packet about a mile off from land. I was informed that she had sunk about 120 kegs. Soon after, as a consequence of becoming intoxicated, the captain and crew ran alongside the *Scourge* cutter. At the time, some of the men were in the act of throwing the remaining kegs overboard. They were floating on the waves, so they were picked up. When the men belonging to the *Scourge* came aboard the packet, they found the captain and two of the sailors quite drunk.

The 120 kegs taken up by the *Scourge* were taken into Exmouth. When they got over the bar [the sand bar covering the mouth of the River Exe at Exmouth], the crew of the packet, promised a reward, turned informers. My partner and the master gave information respecting the rest of the cargo, which the cutter then took up, sharing the money they were given between them. Afterwards they were taken before the magistrates at Exeter. My partner, being a passenger on the vessel, was set free. The captain and one of his men were sent to jail, and after doing me all the injury they could, they then swore that the goods were mine, and that I was the sole proprietor of them. Yet I was only a passenger (the same as my partner, who was cleared), and on shore at the time when the vessel and cargo were taken.

Of all these particulars I was afterward informed, but the intelligence did not reach me in time to be of any benefit, as the sequel shows.

The Lyme Packet was seized early in November 1820. Her master, and part-owner since June 1819, was John Cowley, a Lyme mariner. At the time of her capture, the other owner was Thomas Westlake, described in the Lyme register of shipping as 'a Jersey mariner'. The man released by the magistrates, and therefore the man who was Rattenbury's partner, was William Loveridge. He was probably the same man who crewed for the *Volante* when its boat was seized by Charles Wild four years earlier. Loveridge would have been on board the packet to take bearings when the cargo was sunk. The boy who had accompanied Rattenbury in the rowing boat was Joseph Lobb, who was discharged by the magistrates because he was an apprentice, and because he had not been aboard the vessel when it was taken.

John Cowley and John Brice, one of Cowley's seamen, were consigned to Exeter gaol and it was from there that Cowley, in the hope of being bailed, and of avoiding impressment, offered the collector at Exeter information about Rattenbury.

Cowley said that on Friday 3 November he was at a public house in Weymouth when John Rattenbury came to him saying that he wanted to go to Cherbourg for a cargo of spirits, and would Cowley take him for a freight charge of ten shillings a cask? Cowley first declined, then consented and they sailed from Weymouth on the 6th. On the 8th they arrived at Cherbourg where Rattenbury immediately landed to purchase the goods - 227 casks - which were put on Cowley's vessel on the 9th. That same evening they sailed to Sidmouth where Rattenbury left the vessel saying he was going to procure help to land the cargo. He did not return, and shortly afterwards Cowley's vessel was seized by the *Scourge* cutter under Lt McCrea.

Cowley testified that Rattenbury was the sole owner of the cargo, and that John Brice would corroborate his story if necessary. He further claimed to be unfit for the navy 'having received a serious hurt some time since'. His evidence was placed before the Board on 25 November 1820. Nevertheless, on 19 December, he and Brice were conveyed on board HMS *Impregnable* at Plymouth to be impressed.

Meanwhile, Rattenbury was still smuggling. On 7 December 1820, while anchored off Beer, Lt McCrea, commander of the *Scourge,* wrote to Exeter detailing two related incidents, one relating to Rattenbury. On 2/3 November, a week before the capture of the Lyme Packet, McCrea captured eighty tubs off Otterton Head (probably Otterton Ledge). These might also have belonged to Rattenbury who lost two cargos at about this time. Later on in the month, about ten miles south of Strait Point, McCrea's crew creeped up two rafts, one of 88 tubs, the other of 26 tubs, which he described as being fastened to hawsers and moored with stones. He took them to the Custom House at Topsham. McCrea cruised the same area for sometime afterwards expecting the smugglers to return for their sunken goods, and sure enough, they did - on 29 November. At noon, he observed two boats in the area, both of which appeared to be creeping. One was the *Hannah*. whose master was John Rattenbury. It had been only a week since the loss of the *Elizabeth & Kitty*. This, according to Rattenbury, is what happened next:

> About a fortnight after this melancholy catastrophe, I went to sea in a large open boat, with another man and two of my sons [probably William 19, and John 11] Off Salterton we fell in with the *Scourge* cutter. I did not then know what had been said of me [by Cowley] but was suspicious that all was not right, so I tried my utmost to get away from her, but she saw us and gave chase. She fired her whole eighteen cannon shots at us.

We got on shore, and there found several men from the cutter waiting for us. They had orders from the captain to detain my boat. I said they would not, and took up a large stone which I hove into her intending to stave her. But their numbers were superior, and armed with authority, they at last accomplished their point, took the boat, and towed her into Topsham, where she was laid up in the mud.

By this means I was kept out of employment till the end of December for I had no other boat to go to sea in, which was a great injury to myself and family, particularly at this period. I had suffered so many heavy losses, and my circumstances were in a very declining state.

27. Sidmouth 1833

Something of Rattenbury's desperation at losing his last working boat is felt in the report of the incident made by McCrea, who claimed that, 'an assault on the Crown took place' on Sidmouth beach. This is McCrea's version of what happened after the two smuggling boats were spotted:

> 'On the said boats coming within range of our guns, we hoisted our colors and fired seven shots at them. The northernmost one, named the Concoro(?), bore up and passed under our stern, but the boat Hannah - J Raddenbury master - though one mile further to leeward, and within half gun shot of this cruiser (our shots, eighteen number, dropping in all directions

141

round her), would not bear up but ran on shore between the Peaks near Sidmouth. I sent an officer and boat's crew to examine her. They [found] two creeping ropes and creepers in her and no fishing tackle whatever".

His men were then , said McCrea:

"assailed with the most abusive language, called - in the face of hundreds of the Sidmouth inhabitants, and the officers and crew of the Sidmouth Preventive Boat - murdering beggars, sea robbers, and pirates." [Rattenbury] stripped to fight them, and dashed heavy stones against the boat's bottom with a view to bilging her. [We] hove her off the beach and brought her alongside. Having taken the whole case into consideration, I thought it my duty to detain and send the said boat to Topsham until the pleasure of the Honble Board shall be known." (PRO. Exeter Letterbooks CUST 64/28)

McCrea's report may have strengthened the hand of the collector at Exeter for on 25 January 1821 he informed the Board that he wanted to conduct a 'prosecution against the person mentioned on the back hereof' [ie Rattenbury] 'at the expense of the Crown'. The principal witnesses against him were to be Cowley and Brice.

Rattenbury, unaware of the danger, kept on smuggling.

On 1 January 1821, being then entering the 43rd year of my age [he was 42], I went on board a French vessel with three others as passengers. We went to Cherbourg where we arrived the next day, and took in our cargo. We sailed on the 4th, and on the 5th arrived home with our goods, with which we did very well.

On the 6th, I went to Torquay and joined our vessel

What vessel? Had Rattenbury bought shares in another vessel since the loss of the *Hannah?*

The following day we put to sea with the wind to the eastward. The next day, about a league from Portland, we fell in with the *Greyhound* cutter and the smuggling vessel she had just captured. The commander sent a boat alongside our vessel and took our captain on board the cutter, where he was examined. Find nothing against him, he was dismissed.

About 12 o'clock the same day - the 8th - we saw a brig with her colours up - a signal of distress. We bore down to her and came alongside. She was a Swedish vessel laden with salt and had drifted from her anchor. She was in want of provisions and a pilot. Having parted with what food we could spare, I went on board and offered my services to the captain. He said he wanted to go to Cowes. I said that was impossible because the wind was south-east, but if he wished it, I would undertake to put her into Weymouth or Dawlish.

After a little consideration he decided in favour of Weymouth, which was the nearest, and agreed to give me £80 for my assistance. We then made all the sail we could, and in three and a half hours we were in Weymouth roads. There another pilot came on board with the agent. Having left a young man that was with me behind, I returned to our vessel, and we proceeded on our voyage [Rattenbury's vessel having accompanied the Swedish vessel to Weymouth].

The next morning, about day-break, we fell in with an Indiaman which supplied us with such provisions as we were in need of.

On the following day, the 11th, we arrived at Cherbourg, took in our cargo, and sailed on the 13th. We got home with our goods, part of which we afterwards lost, but we saved enough to do pretty well.

On 29 January we went again as passengers to France. We returned with a cargo consisting of a hundred kegs of spirits, and a bale of tea. We worked down with another smuggling vessel, which was bound to Exmouth harbour. About a league or more off Budleigh Salterton, we wound away, got out our boat, put all the goods into her, and veered the boat astern. Five minutes later we saw a boat. We recognised it as a king's boat, so we cut away our boat from the stern.

The king's boat came alongside of us, and the captain attempted to come on board, but we told him to keep off. They again attempted to board us, and when we shoved the boat off with a boat-hook, they dropped astern of our vessel and began to fire at us. The first shot carried away our main halliards [halyards] and down came the sail. She rode up again under the stern, and when they renewed the fire, one of our men hove a shy-stone at the boat. It pitched on the gunnel [gunwhale]. Still they kept firing, and several shots went through the counter and companions of our vessel. They continued to fire till their ammunition was quite exhausted, then they rode up alongside.

"What do you want?" I asked.

The commander recollected my voice. 'Master Rattenbury, you had better let me come alongside quietly."

I prevailed on the crew, English and French, to let him do so. He came on board and searched the vessel but found nothing. I then asked him to take refreshments, which he did. He enquired about the other vessel [ie the smuggling vessel bound for Exmouth]. I told him it was a pilot sloop.

Whilst they were with me, our vessel ran alongside the boat we had cut away, the one laden with our goods. Our crew were obliged to shove her off with a boat-hook to prevent her discovery. Soon afterwards, they became so very mutinous that I have every reason to believe dreadful consequences would have ensued had it not been for my interference.

Captain Stocker, who was the commander, remained till 3 o'clock in the morning when, having no plea for detaining the vessel, he left. He was about twenty yards away when he called out to me.

'Mind, Mr Rattenbury, if I find you and your vessel here in the morning, I'll detain you."

A fine breeze sprang up from the NNW and we cruised about in search of our boat, but could not find her. The next morning, at daybreak, a long way off, we saw Captain Stocker with two Salterton boats, They had our boat - the one containing our goods - in tow.

We made our way to Beer but returned to France the same day for fear of being apprehended. We remained there a fortnight, then came home with a cargo. I then went on shore and sent a crew off to the vessel to secure the goods, but about 10 o'clock at night, when the wind was blowing very hard ENE, a tremendous sea hauled the stern of the boat out. The next morning the crew came on shore and gave an account of their accident. I then went cruising for the tubs, but a gale obliged me to run ashore at Sidmouth, while the best of our goods were driven on shore at Penton [Paignton], near Torbay.

Stocker was a problem for Rattenbury but it was Richard Morgan, the mate of the *Scourge* cutter, whom he had most to fear from because Morgan had been given the responsibility of apprehending him for his part in the Lyme Packet affair.

In February, as I was on the cliffs on the look-out, I saw the mate of the *Scourge*. The night before I had heard that he was enquiring after me so I went up to him and asked what he wanted.

'I have a spyglass belonging to you. If you come on board the cutter, I'll give it to you."

After a little more conversation we parted. I then took my boat and with my two little boys [John 11, and Abraham 4], went on board. When I arrived, I was told that the mate was at breakfast with another person, so I sent my little boys below. After waiting some time on deck, I went down also. I was on board about an hour before the mate sent for me. When I went into his cabin, a deputation officer was there with another man. The mate took out a writ which had been issued against me in consequence of the information given by Cowley, the captain of the Lyme packet. Having read it, the deputation officer said that I was his prisoner.

I can't describe how I felt at finding I had been trepanned [ensnared] in such a manner. When the deputation officer desired me to go below, I positively declared that I would not. One of the men asked me what I was going to do with the boys? The question so goaded me that, in a rage, I replied: 'Throw them overboard if you like and drown them. You might just as well, having taken their father from them, and in such a clandestine manner!"

I asked the mate to let me go on shore and try to get bail, but the fine was such a large one - £4500 - that he told me it was not in his power. He then sent my two little boys on shore. Half an hour later, when the boat returned, we made all sail for Exmouth. At about 2 o'clock we got to the foot of the bar and the mate sent me below with the deputation officer and steward till we arrived [at Exmouth]. Then he came below himself.

"You may go on deck if you please," he said.

There I met the captain [Robert McCrea], who had just come on board. I addressed him on the subject of my arrest.

"I know nothing about it," he said. "It is all Cowley's concern."

I was then taken on shore where a coach was waiting. Into it got the mate, the deputation officer, and myself. One of the men belonging to the cutter was outside as a guard. He was well armed.

When we reached Exeter I was taken under a very strong escort to the sheriff's office. They were armed with pistols so it was impossible for me to make any effort to escape. At the sheriff's office I again proposed putting in bail, but was told it would not be worth while as the writ would be out in two days, and then I would have to find special bail. That same day I was removed to St Thomas's ward [a prison in Exeter], where I found my situation less uncomfortable than I expected.

At the ensuing assizes, I employed Mr Cox the attorney, and Mr Tyrrell the barrister, to carry on a trial against the government because the writ had been served on the high seas. I paid them £68, but lost the trial.

Being now in great distress, I was engaged as a servant to the insolvent debtors till 9 August when, through an act of grace passed by his gracious majesty George IV, I once more obtained my liberty and returned home, where I was joyfully received by my wife and family.

On his arrest Rattenbury was conveyed by coach from Exmouth to Exeter where, on 10 February 1821, he was committed to the prison of St Thomas the Apostle to await trial. On 17 March he petitioned Customs for the allowance normally granted to extremely poor prisoners. The keeper at the gaol, Charles Boutcher, approved his petition saying that Rattenbury was entitled to it 'he being poor and having no property to support him, and further he is confined in the suit of the Revenue of the Customs only'.

His trial did not take place until the first week of June. It was held in London where he was taken, under guard, in a coach hired for the purpose. The two men who were his counsel were probably from Lyme - attorney Samuel H Cox of Market Place, and barrister John Tyrell of 24 Fore St.

At about the time of Rattenbury's trial, Morgan, the mate of the *Scourge* cutter, was asked by the Board why it was that he and McCrea resorted so often to hiring coaches (at the Board's expense) to transport smugglers from Exmouth to Exeter when other methods - by boat up the Exe, or public conveyance - were available? Morgan explained that, on both the occasions referred to by the Board, the number of prisoners involved - four in November and six in February - and the speed of dispatch had been important. When the *Scourge* had arrived at Exmouth with the prisoners, the hour had been late, the public conveyance had already left town, and taking the prisoners by water would have meant waiting for the canal locks to open. The cutter and its crew did not want to be detained at Exmouth longer than necessary - there being no other revenue cutter available to patrol the coast in its stead - so they had resorted to coach hire. The collector at Exeter accepted Morgan's explanation, and endorsed it in a reply to the Board.

Although Rattenbury was convicted in June 1821 and sent to prison, he does not say where, but it likely to have been the Devon County Gaol in Exeter. Most smugglers caught within the jurisdiction of Exeter Customs were sent there. So what was the gaol like?

In the *Exeter Flying Post* of 21 December 1820, a summary was published stating the numbers of prisoners held, their food allowances, and the work they were expected to perform. Between Autumn 1819 and Autumn 1820, 1,834 prisoners were processed, each entitled to a daily allowance of 22 ounces of 'best Wheaten bread', and one pound of bacon per week 'not exceeding in value One Penny per Day - convicted Felons and Misdemeanors, each Prisoner Half a Peck of Potatoes per Week, additional'. It continues:

> *"Every prisoner is employed. Those whose commitments are not for labor, are entitled to one-half of their earnings. Such as are committed for hard labor are not entitled by law to any share of what they earn, but they are here allowed, as an encouragement to industry, one-fourth part, which is paid them on their discharge.*
>
> *Besides the Keeper's House, Chapel, &c, this Bridewell is divided into six Wings, or distinct Prisons, for keeping separate and apart the different classes of Prisoners. There are likewise six Airing Grounds, with Work-Shops, and a very extensive Court-Yard, for carrying on a variety of laborious Employments, such as Sawing and Polishing Marble, Sawing and Sanding Stone, Pumping, Beating Hemp, Pounding Oyster Shells, Picking Oakum, Shoemaking, Tayloring, Lace-making, Plaiting Straw, Washing, Making and Mending, Manufacturing Flax,... also Spinning, Heckling, Spooling, Warping and Weaving the same into Piece."*

Rattenbury says he was released on 9 August, but does not give the year. If it was the same year as his trial, then he served a sentence of barely two months, which seems strangefc given the trouble to which Customs had gone to capture, convict, and imprison him. So how long was he in prison for?

CHAPTER 17

Smuggling and Preventive Measures
1821-1825

1820, the year of Rattenbury's escapade aboard the Lyme Packet, was a peak year for the number of men employed by the Government on preventive duties. Their salaries alone were costing £500,000 a year, which cancelled out the value of any seizures. Their efforts were largely dissipated by lack of co-ordination because the Admiralty controlled the revenue vessels while Customs controlled everything else. There was too a lack of communication between Customs outports, and this allowed dedicated smugglers like Rattenbury the freedom to move their operations from one area to another without being readily recognised. Under Admiralty control, the turnover of cutter commanders was rapid and it was not unusual for entire crews to be dismissed. Lost with them was the knowledge of local smugglers they had built up.

In 1822 these problems were acknowledged and many of the changes made to the revenue service in 1816 were reversed, the waterguard (the boatmen), the land guard (the 3000 riding officers), and the revenue vessels (which were reduced in number), being brought together under the solo control of Customs to form the coastguard. However, the cutter commanders continued to be selected from royal navy personnel.

This unified approach was more effective, but what helped the new coastguard most was improved intelligence. If cutter commanders could find out which vessels were loading contraband at ports like Roscoff and Cherbourg, then they also knew which to try to intercept, so some revenue vessels were sent on intelligence-gathering missions.

We do not know if the formation of the coastguard had an impact on Rattenbury's smuggling activities from 1822 to 1825 because neither he, nor they, have anything to say about them during the period. However, his son and other Beer men were keeping them busy. In January 1821, Daniel French had a narrow escape when his vessel, the *Juliana,* was detained in Guernsey on suspicion of smuggling. No contraband was found on her so she was released but John Radford, a Guernsey customs official, was in no doubt whatsoever of French's intentions, describing him as a professed smuggler.

A month later William Abbot, Timothy Marley and John Steple were smuggling and had the misfortune to be drowned during a landing. Their fate was noted in the Beer and Seaton parish register on 26 February 1821.

The frequent changes of senior personnel aboard revenue cutters hindered the anti-smuggling effort, but it continued. Soon after Rattenbury's capture, Lt McCrea left the *Scourge* and was replaced by Lt Daniel Weld. On 6 August 1821, Weld boarded the *Concent* of Beer, owned by William Smith who was aboard. With Smith were Robert Bartlett, Robert Smith and John Loveridge. The five kegs and the canister of tea which had been thrown overboard were picked up by the men of the revenue cutter. Two of the kegs were clearly marked with the names of William Smith and Robert Bartlett. A year later William Smith, Henry Hetchley, John Woodgate, and James Smith, were drowned in a smuggling vessel on the coast of France.

Also in 1822 Richard Broadbridge seized 27 casks of foreign spirits from in and around the house of John Gill of Colyton, believed to be an agent for smugglers in the neighbourhood. In September of the same year, Isaac Tidbury and five other men were caught off Beer by the *Scourge* cutter and carried into Exmouth.

On 11 January 1823, Beer boatman John Hawkins had an encounter at the eastern extremity of Seaton Beach with James Haycraft of Seaton, a noted carrier of smuggled goods, but a much more serious incident occurred three days later. Lt John Morgan RN, working with the Beer boatmen, was on the lookout at Seaton Bay when he spied parties of men going to the assistance of a boat. He hid and watched. A group of men laden with tubs were about to pass him when he stopped them and seized six tubs. As a result, about fifty smugglers, some armed with bludgeons, came up and, swearing and cursing, started to throw large stones at him. One stone struck Morgan in the groin; another caught him in the ribs. Morgan recognised William Power and declared his name out loud, which caused the whole party to retreat leaving him in possession of the tubs; but they came on again, beat him with sticks, and took the tubs back. Although in extreme pain from the blows, he went in search of help from Richard Broadbridge.

William Power was arrested and sent for trial which made Morgan so unpopular in Seaton where he lived that on 16 May he had to leave in fear of his life.

The day after the incident on the beach, the crew of the coastguard boat at Beer, under their new chief officer, Robert Aldrich, seized the *Agenona* of Beer with 26 casks aboard. Abraham Sydenham was captured but the rest of the crew escaped. Sydenham was fined £100 but was unable to pay. At 70 years old he was also unfit for the navy so he was sent to Dorchester Prison where, nearly a year later, the keeper reported that he was in poor health and spirits.

Abraham Sydenham had been one of Rattenbury's associates. So had William Dominy, imprisoned in Dorchester in October 1825. He too was penniless. Confirmation of Dominy's smuggling past is contained in a report dated 15 April 1823 when customs officials described him as having been the part-owner - along with William Fox of Lyme - of a vessel which had been seized for smuggling tobacco in May 1815.

William Rattenbury was caught again just off Beer on 11 July 1823 when Robert Aldrich seized 94 casks in the *Mary* of Beer. Aboard were five men, all of whom were declared fit for naval service and who, on conviction, were sent to Dorchester prison and later impressed. Apart from William 21, there was James Taylor of Bristol, James Macnamara 28, originally of Cork but belonging to Beer, Charles Hurrell 31, and John Snell of Branscombe, 28. Over a year later, on 29 September 1825, Aldrich claimed expenses of over £7 for having taken William Rattenbury from Dorchester gaol to Portsmouth to be impressed.

Confined in Dorchester Prison the same year as William Rattenbury were other men from the Beer area: William Loveridge 63 (another of Rattenbury's former partners), Jacob Lane 58, John Drew 48, John Rowe 55, Samuel Cox 56, and James Webber of Budleigh Salterton. Loveridge, Lane and Webber had been captured together. Jacob Lane was distinguished by a tattoo on his left arm which listed the names of his entire family: 'Jacob Lane, John Lane, Susanna Lane, Isaac Lane, Sarah Lane, a mermaid, Mary Lane, Elizabeth Lane, 1794'.

The reference to John Drew as a smuggler is interesting because, in March 1820 a revenue cutter crewman of the same name was dismissed for misconduct by Lt McCrea of the *Scourge*. McCrea later claimed that, to get his revenge, Drew had spread untruths in Beer about John Peek, another *Scourge* crew member and former sitter of the Beer boat. Was it the same John Drew I wonder?

The Beer and Seaton fishermen and seamen who languished in Dorchester prison in 1824 and 1825 were Samuel Miller 49, William Manley 46, Richard Driver 43, and William Driver 13. The eldest, however, was none other than Daniel French 67 who, according to the prison records, wore a wig!

Dorchester prison had a smugglers' ward and in 1825 the governor complained that he had 'found a great degree of difficulty in introducing sobriety of thought, and exciting attention to religious instruction among the smugglers, from a feverish state of mind prevalent in that class of prisoner'. But prison was better than a watery grave, which was the fate of John Collier, John Sydenham, Jabez Rutter and two Frenchmen in December 1824.

A year earlier an interesting situation arose which not only throws light on small transactions in smuggled alcohol in Beer itself, but stimulates conjecture about the relationship of the two people involved. William Cox, a constable of the parish of Seaton and Beer, offered to the collector at Lyme information against Sarah Caddy, a Beer widow of some property, saying that she had asked him to procure for her a 2s 3d bottle of smuggled goods. This he did on 15 October 1823, getting it from a cask brought back from France. But the Board was less interested in Mrs Caddy's purchase of a bottle of contraband spirits than Cox's knowledge of the existence and whereabouts of the cask he decanted it from! They recommended to the collector and controller at Lyme that they:

> "call upon William Cox to state from whom he obtained the brandy which he sold to Sarah Caddy, and how he knew that the same had been brought from France and that duty had not been paid upon it. The Collector and Comptroller may also enquire the motives which induced Cox to give this information, and whether Sarah Caddy bears the character of a Dealer in Smuggled Spirits. Also whether Cox can bring forward any person to corroborate his statement."

The collector and comptroller followed the Board's advice and reported back to them on 31 December 1823:

> "We called on Cox, who is unwilling to state from whom he obtained the Brandy. He says it was brought to him direct from a Boat but by whom he will not mention, though he can swear positively that the duty was never paid. We are unable to discover what motives actuated him to lay this information, but we are given to understand that he is the tenant of Sarah Caddy, and we suspect there must be some private pique against her. She has the character of being a Dealer in smuggled spirits. Cox is unwilling to bring forward anyone to corroborate his statement, and we have no doubt that he is himself connected with the smugglers." (PRO. Lyme Letterbooks CUST 63/3)

Many are the statements made by customs officers, and in petitions by smugglers, which stimulate the imagination without satisfying it, but none more so than those relating to William Cox and the widow Caddy. One can only speculate on the nature of a relationship which resulted in the one trying to get the other into serious trouble; and possibly into prison.

In Beer, William Cox knew where one cask of contraband spirits was kept, but it can't have been the only one hidden there given the state of smuggling in the Lyme area in late 1823 and early 1824, which was summed up in a report to the Board on 3 February 1824:

> "From all the information we are enabled to procure on the subject, we are of the opinion that a considerable increase has

taken place in smuggling within our Port, and your Honors may be able to judge the extent to which this trade is carried on from the circumstance of 2s/3d being the usual retail price for a bottle of brandy. The mode of smuggling has not varied from that described in our letter of 23 March. In this part of the coast it requires time and experience to gain a local knowledge of the haunts and practices of the smugglers, so we cannot but consider these perpetual changes in the boatmen attached to the Preventive Water Guard, as very impolitic, and of serious detriment to the service. " (PRO. Lyme Letterbooks CUST 63/3)

The Lyme customs letterbooks are peppered with the names of Beer smugglers, but few receive the special mentions earned by John and William Rattenbury, and by William Gibbs. In 1824, Gibbs was on a Beer boat boarded about seven miles off Lyme by the Lyme coastguard. Nothing was found on board but a small cask and two hawsers yet according to the chief officer, James Scott, Gibbs violently obstructed and assaulted his men, actually striking three with the boat's tiller and with his fist. Gibbs was taken before the magistrate and bound over to appear before the next Dorset county assizes. The other four men, having conducted themselves peacefully, were liberated. The Lyme collector described Gibbs as 'a most notorious smuggler and one of the most violent characters on the coast'.

In December 1824, the sloop *Daniel* of Portsmouth, her boat, and 132 casks were seized by Robert Aldrich, and the names of her crew - Samuel Cox, Samuel Miller, William Gibbs, and Thomas Green - were entered in the Lyme letterbook; but it was not until December 1825 that the name of John Rattenbury reappeared in similar records, and then it was not for activities in the Lyme area, but for those around Exeter.

CHAPTER 18

From Exeter Gaol to Westminster
1825-1830

When I got a little settled [after coming out of gaol], I again engaged in smuggling, fishing and piloting. On December 1825, as I was returning from a smuggling expedition, I was captured off Dawlish by the crew of a boat belonging to the coastguard, and carried to Budleigh Salterton watch house. There I remained until 2 January 1826, when an order arrived from the Board to take me before the magistrates, who committed me to Exeter jail.

28. Budleigh Salterton 1830

The five-man crew of a boat called *Mary* were convicted of smuggling on 3 January 1826 and sent to Devon County Gaol in Exeter. One - William Tozer - was impressed into the navy.

It was common for poor prisoners to petition the Customs Board for an allowance, and in January 1826 this was done by several smugglers, some of whose names are already familiar - Abraham and William Sydenham, William Woodgate and John Newton. John Potter of Branscombe had been apprehended by the Beer coastguard. All were granted gaol allowances, as was John Rattenbury when he applied:

> Not being satisfied with the jail allowance - 22 ounces of bread every morning, 10lbs of potatoes and 1lb of pork per week - I wrote a letter to the Board for my pay instead. As a result, on 15 February, an order was received that I was to be paid 4½d per day.

Rattenbury was in prison for over a year, during which time smuggling in the Beer area eased off, largely as a result of the increasing effectiveness of the coastguard. Suspicious vessels were readily confiscated, as happened on 14 November 1827 when Lt Brown, chief officer of the Beer coastguard, seized a Beer boat called the *Black-Eyed Maid*. Brown suspected that, along with the *Speculator*, also of Beer, she had been smuggling. He could not prove it and therefore detained her on a legal technicality - being at sea with more hands than she was licensed for.

John Miller, the owner and master of the *Black-Eyed Maid*, enlisted the aid of N T Still Esq, a well-to-do tenant of Lord Rolle's, in an attempt to get her back. Miller insisted that Henry Gibbs, the 12-year old boy Lt Brown identified as the fifth hand, was not part of her crew, but had been on board only because the *Maid* was bringing him back to Beer for medical attention. William Gibbs had also been on board the *Maid*. The crew of the *Speculator* - Henry Miller, Thomas Driver, William Bartlett and Henry Newton - were witnesses too, and all four swore before B J Stuckey Bartlett, the Branscombe magistrate, that what Miller said was true. Miller's petition was sent to the Treasury accompanied by a supportive letter from Mr Still:

> *"As resident on Lord Rolle's property in the parish of Beer, I respectfully beg to enclose an affidavit relative to the seizure of a fishing boat which appears a case of great hardship, as the sole reason for which the boat was detained arose from an act of humanity in conveying on shore a little boy whose hand had been injured, and who had suffered greatly from being exposed two nights to rain and severe weather. In making this representation I cannot but advert not only to the case of the individuals, who are thus thrown out of employ, but to the expense this detention is likely to occasion in a parish where, from a general scarcity of labour, the poor rates are excessively burthensome, and the want of boats for fishing is a most ferocious evil."*

Lt Brown, asked by the Board to give his reason for seizing the *Black-Eyed Maid*, replied:

"She is a boat well known to have been in general use for the purposes of smuggling, and I firmly believe - from her having on board slung stones and other suspicious circumstances - that she had (in connection with the Speculator *galley), been so employed immediately previous to her seizure.*

With reference to the statement of the crew, and of N T Still, Esq, that the boy was brought on shore for surgical aid. I must beg leave to observe that I have strong reasons for supposing that such was not the cause of the boy being in the boat, first because it did not appear to me that the said boy had sustained any injury whatever, and second because they had stated to me that their reason for bringing him on shore was his being seasick, not on account of any wound in his hand, as they now state."

Lt Brown went on to point out further contradictions in the testimony of the fishermen, and concluded:

"I come now to the character of the parties, all of whom have been in the constant practice of smuggling. Three out of the six have been (and more than once), convicted of that offence, which makes it appear that they are not altogether deserving of the levity solicited for them by N T Still Esq. Be that as it may, seeing that a fifth hand is of so decided an advantage to the smuggler, I have felt myself called on to enforce the Act of Parliament which restricts vessels and boats to limited crews." (PRO. Lyme Letterbooks CUST 63/5)

Miller had been advised by Still and others that he had grounds for a civil action against Lt Brown because the seizure of the boat had been both oppressive and illegal, but the collector at Lyme supported Brown, so Miller did not get his boat back. Later on in this chapter, Rattenbury refers to a Major Still. It may have been the same man.

Between 1825 and 1830 a steady stream of Beer smugglers were captured and sent to Dorchester and Exeter prisons. They included John Mills 42, Thomas Miller, Thomas Bartlett, John Newton, James Bools, Robert Gush and Richard Horsford. For the apprehension of the last four, Robert Aldrich the chief officer at Beer, claimed a reward of four guineas each.

On 18 October 1826 Exeter customs filed a half-yearly report on smuggling, pointing out that, although the trade had met with severe setbacks, it was far from being crushed, and that a new party of smugglers was operating to the west of the Exe because of the increasing difficulty of landing cargos on beaches to the east of it. Few direct runs had been made, the system still being to sink the goods first; although the coastguard had swept for and found some of the casks themselves. Beer smugglers were, of course, suspected.

There was little smuggling throughout the summer of 1826, but it resumed in the winter, and on 20 December Malachi Partridge and William Loveridge were apprehended at Budleigh Salterton with a small quantity of contraband spirits. They were committed to Devon County Gaol where on 12 February 1827 the keeper, William Cole, testified that they were both poor men with families and thus entitled to an allowance. Albert Cox, caught with them, was sent to Plymouth for impressment.

There is no doubt that the officers of the coastguard of the 1820s were more alert and more effective than their predecessors of 1815 and 1816. Suspicious transactions and characters were diligently recorded for future reference. For example, on 21 October 1826, when Elias Horsford of Beer was granted a licence for his new open boat the *Malt Bag*, it was noted that local officers believed it would be used for smuggling because Horsford was a 'very suspicious character'.

Whether Elias Horsford did smuggle in his *Malt Bag* is not known. Nor is it known which Beer men Exeter customs believed were helping in operations west of the Exe, but it was unlikely to have been John Rattenbury, who was still languishing in prison.

> I had been in prison about nine months when, one morning, while the governor was in the hospital, one of the transports [a convict who had been sentenced to be transported], with whom together with others who were in to take their trial for every description of crime I was most unpleasantly associated, gave him a blow on the head with a brush. The governor was felled to the floor senseless, and they all ran down into the day-room. The turnkeys gave the alarm, and myself and the other smugglers assisted in securing them before they had effected their escape. Because of this, the governor wrote a petition to the board on our behalf, but it was of no benefit to us.

There is no doubt that this is the incident reported in the *Exeter Flying Post* on 13 May 1824, under the title of 'Ferocious Attack on the Governor of Devon County Gaol':

> *'In our last [report] we noted the daring attempts at escape and riotous conduct of several felons confined in the County Gaol. The same disorderly conduct continued - to the great disturbance of the other inmates of the prison - through the night of Saturday last when Toms, and a prisoner named William Thomas (alias Oram, against whom sentence of Death had also been recorded at the last Assizes), persisted in calling loudly to each other, by which means (though in different divisions), a conversation was kept up.*
> *With a view to getting rid of this annoyance, Mr Cole on Sunday morning gave orders to change their cells and place them in parts of the building so remote as to prevent the possibility of*

their holding communication. This was effected with regard to Thomas, but resisted with dreadful imprecations by Toms. And Mr Cole, going himself to enforce it, was struck senseless to the floor by a blow on the forehead from a brush, with which the miscreant had armed himself. Slipping from his jacket, which he left in the hands of the turnkeys who had seized him, he [Toms] bolted over the stairs to the day room, calling on the other prisoners to join him, which some of those confined for serious offences seemed disposed to do.

But the others - those [there] for misdemeanours and for offences against the Excise Laws - to their great credit, immediately volunteered their services in support of the Governor and his assistants, and rendered effectual aid in securing their refractory comrades. Thomas Combstock, a prisoner of the latter description, received some very severe blows in the contest.

During this alarming state of things, the prison bell had been rung, on hearing which the 14th Dragoons in the Barracks turned out with a celerity and promptitude that reflects the greatest credit on the Officers and Men of this highly disciplined Regiment. A party of them now arriving at the prison, the desperate villains were secured.

Such is the high estimation in which Mr Cole the governor is held that the injury he received has caused a general feeling of regret, and we feel great pleasure in being able to state that he is recovering from the effect of it.

There are now in the Gaol eighteen prisoners against whom sentence of death was recorded at the last Assize, but which was afterwards commuted for other punishments. It appears that there are among them several of a more violent and daring character than are often met with, even in prisons. In the almost constant state of mutiny which their conduct has exhibited, they have been influenced, as they declare, by the idea that let their conduct be what it may in the Gaol, they can undergo no other punishment than transportation for life, to which they are already sentenced. After securing Toms in a solitary cell, the visiting magistrate, S F Milford Esq, has therefore informed them that if they are guilty of any further violence, he will immediately order for each of them a severe flagellation, to be repeated as often as they persevere in their outrages. This unexpected information appears to have had the desired effect, and tranquillity seems to be restored."

I do not know why Rattenbury dates this event two years after the time it actually happened. As there is no reason to suppose he was lying about his involvement, he must have been a prisoner in Exeter gaol in May 1824 when the incident occurred. There can be only two explanations for this: either his capture at Budleigh Salterton occurred two years before he says it did, or he was still serving the sentence imposed upon him in June 1821 for his part in the Lyme packet affair. Far from being imprisoned for a few months, he may have been imprisoned for several years. Indeed, he may have spent most of the time between February 1821 and April 1827 in incarceration. Unfortunately most of the archives relating to Devon County Gaol have not survived so this theory cannot be easily checked.

> About three months after this I sent a letter to Sir William Pole. He kindly wrote on my behalf to the lords of the Treasury, who sent word that fifteen months from the date of my trial, I might be set at liberty. Accordingly, on 5 April 1827, Mr Hull, accompanied by the collector of the customs, called at the governor's house, and I signed a bond for £500. Through the goodness of God, and the influence of kind friends, I was once more free. I immediately returned to my family at Beer.

Rattenbury's family now consisted of William 26, Frances 22, John 18, Ann 14, Abraham 11, Mary Ann 8, and Elizabeth 5. William was married, having wed Susannah Clarke on 21 July 1921. John's eighth and final child Hannah, born in 1828, was conceived soon after his release from Exeter gaol.

Sir William Pole was a baronet who lived at Shute House, Colyton, only a mile or two from Beer. The house was built in 1787. Not long after, in 1794, the Rev John Swete saw it when travelling through East Devon:

> 'Quitting Colcombe Caste I rode up a long steep hill to the North to the new house of Shute. This was erected, or rather begun, in 1787 by the present representative of the Pole Family who, in the year 1789, by the king's permission, took himself the name of de la Pole... The South Front is of good height being four storeys, and the site chosen for the prospect which it commanded. In the utmost perfection, the rich and finely wooded valley are expanded to the East and West and terminate in the villages of Axmouth and Seaton." (Devon Record Office, 564M)

In 1827, de la Pole was involved, with others, in the Grand Western Canal Company which was considering a project to build a canal to complete an inland waterway between the Bristol and English Channels. Since Roman times the mouths of the Axe and the Otter have gradually silted up, leaving the east Devon coast without a harbour. Several attempts were made to unblock them, and when that failed ideas were floated about building a harbour in the area. According to M G Dickinson in *A Living from the Sea*, Acts of Parliament for a harbour at Beer were passed in 1792 and 1820, without any action to build one being taken. The issue was revived again in 1827. Evidence on sea conditions off the east Devon coast was to be submitted to a committee of enquiry for the House of Commons. No-one knew that coast better than its most notorious smuggler, John Rattenbury, who had just been released from prison.

29. Shute House, near Colyton 1794

About the latter end of May, the Rev Dr Palmer, Major Still, and Major Pine sent for me to attend them at Colyton, which I did. They wanted me to go to London concerning the harbour then being contemplated for Beer, and the grand western canal which was to extend from Beer to Thorverton, a distance of 42 miles. To this proposal I readily consented. Dr Palmer then gave me a guinea and asked me to call at Mr Sampson's at 8 o'clock next morning, which I did. The doctor took me in his gig to Shute House where we alighted. After about half an hour, Sir William Pole came to the door.

'Here is Rob Roy come again,' he said. He ordered me into the house to take refreshments, and treated me very kindly.

From Shute House we proceeded to Chard, where I remained at an inn till the following morning when Mr Salter, the solicitor's clerk, called for me to go to London by the mail. We arrived there about 11 o'clock the next morning.

On the ensuing day, I was desired to attend at the Western Canal Office, from which place I went with others to Westminster Hall where I saw Lord Rolle. He ordered me to attend there every day till I was called, which was not until 14 June. During all that time I received one guinea per day and had all my expenses paid, so I was well pleased.

The counsellor who examined me in the House of Commons asked me what trade I followed. I told him sometimes fishing, sometimes piloting, and sometimes smuggling. Sir Isaac Coffin asked me several questions concerning the depth of the sea at various parts of the bay from Portland to Start Point, how I would get vessels round Portland in a gale of wind SSW, and whether I had seen a great many vessels lost through not having a harbour, to which I answered in the affirmative.

My examination lasted about three quarters of an hour, and I explained as best I could everything relative to the subject. I was told that I conducted myself very well. On the following morning, I went to the agent's office and received the money due to me. I immediately took a place in the coach and returned in high spirits to my family.

I had been home about a fortnight when I engaged in a smuggling expedition. It was accomplished in a week, but on returning we were chased by the *Invincible* cutter. Night came on so we escaped. We sunk the kegs, but lost them through a man informing against us.

On 2 July, Lord Rolle sent for me to go to the House of Lords concerning the canal and harbour. I immediately obeyed the summons and arrived in London in two days. The next morning I went to Westminster Hall where I saw Lord R and Dr Palmer. They again asked me to attend every day till I was called, which I promised to do. I then went to the Western Canal Office where I received £5.

On the third day, I was called to give evidence in the House of Lords. After the oath had been administered I was examined and cross-examined. To the best of my ability, I explained everything I was required to.

The next morning I went to Grosvenor Square, Lord Rolle having desired me to call at his house. He gave me half a guinea and told me to go to the office for my money, which I did. I received twice as much as before and returned home with blue ribbons in my hat and a merry heart, for I expected to derive great advantage from the passing of the act. In this I was sadly disappointed. Although the bill was passed, the project was dropped entirely.

Lord Rolle appears to have taken an interest in Rattenbury and to have acted as his patron, and it is through his good offices that the smuggler, at the age of 51, obtained a post as a crewman aboard - of all things - a revenue cutter!

I remained at home engaged in my old occupations until the year 1829, when I made an application to Lord R, who gave me a letter to the admiral at Portsmouth. I went on board the *Tartar* cutter and stayed there two months. I then went to the admiral's office where I received an order to go on board the admiral's ship, but I didn't like it and so returned to the *Tartar* cutter then at Cowes. I remained on board as a seaman until 10 November when I was taken ill and put on shore at Beer. Within a week the cutter came after me, and carried me to Weymouth, where I was placed in sick quarters till 6 January 1830.

Lieutenant Watson was on the point of leaving the *Tartar* and I applied to him for my discharge, which he gave me. I then went to the custom house for my pay. I went home, where I remained until March when I went in a trade to London to meet two of my sons [William would have been 28, John 20 and Abraham 13] on their arrival from Scotland. After staying a week, they set out on another voyage.

I returned to Beer and employed myself in fishing, etc, until new year's day when I called on Lord R. He was very angry with me for leaving the cutter. He told me if I was ill he could have procured a long leave of absence, but now he would do nothing more for me. I then called upon several gentlemen to whom I was known. They each gave me a new year's gift, by which means I and my family were made very comfortable.

What an interesting little custom. Rattenbury, short of money, simply went round asking for it from 'gentlemen' known to him. Were these the same gentlemen who were his contacts in the Grand Western Canal affair? Had they purchased contraband of him? Lord Rolle had been his first target, but it seems that all he gave Rattenbury was a dressing down!

CHAPTER 19

Scottish Travels; Dorchester Prison
1830-1834

Rattenbury, now in his fifties, was surely finding that his notoriety as a smuggler was making it difficult for him to operate as one. He may have had to take whatever employment he could get, which is why in February 1830 we find him as the mate of a trading vessel not its master, and sailing in conditions which were far from ideal.

In February 1830, I sailed from Lyme as mate of a schooner bound for Topsham with half a cargo of wheat. Having discharged our load, we proceeded to Exeter and took in a cargo of manganese for Kilmarnock in Scotland. On 10 March, with only three men and a boy - one of whom met with an accident that prevented him carrying out his duties - we sailed down the canal, sailing over Exmouth bar on the 11th. For seven nights I remained on deck. On the 18th, the wind was blowing so hard from the east we were obliged to put in at Shields, where we stayed four days. There we left our disabled hand in hospital and got a another to replace him.

On the 22nd we continued on our voyage, arriving at our destined port on the 28th. We discharged our cargo and I informed the captain that I wished to leave the vessel and go to Banff to see my sons, so he paid me my wages and gave me a good character.

I had a very fine passage to Spa [?] in a smack, and proceeded from thence to Banff by land, but my sons did not arrive till a few days afterwards. I stayed with them and shipped myself on board a little vessel of 40 tons, which was carrying salmon to Aberdeen. I belonged to her for two months, and then engaged in the herring fishery, in which I was very successful. When this was over, I embarked with my sons for London, where we arrived after five days. I remained with them until they set out on another voyage, and then returned home to Beer at the latter end of August.

The fishing link between Devon and Scotland is interesting because the trawlers developed in Brixham were of the type which later formed the large fishing fleets based on the north-east coast of Britain.

Rattenbury does not tell us which two of his three sons were involved in the Scottish fishing and coasting trade, but it was probably John 21 and Abraham 14. Unlike their brother William, their names do not appear in the local customs records as smugglers, and there is no reason to believe that they were ever involved. Their employment in the Scottish fishing industry kept them away from

Beer. They may have formed relationships so far away that they never had cause to return permanently to their home parish.

John Rattenbury was back in Beer in 1831, the same year in which the coastguard again underwent alterations, the men who served now being regarded as part of the naval reserve. Not only the cutter commanders were to be naval lieutenants, so too were the chief officers of the coastguard stations. In Beer, Lt Buxton became the chief officer.

On 4 January 1831, I observed a vessel about four leagues off from Beer. Her colours were flying for a pilot so I got a boat and rowed off to her. She was a Dutchman which had sailed from Alexandria and was bound to Amsterdam. She had mistaken the Portland light for that of the Gaskets [the Casquets, in the Channel Islands?]. The captain agreed to give me £15 for carrying her into Exmouth harbour. The vessel was so leaky and foul we rode quarantine five days, then the Dutch agent paid me and I returned home.

One day in September, returning home after I had been fishing three leagues from land, a violent gale of wind arose from the south-west. A heavy sea broke over the boat and washed a sail overboard, carrying me with it. One of the other men caught hold of the yard, and the sea hove me back into the boat, which was going at the rate of five or six knots an hour. Thus was I preserved from a watery grave.

At the latter end of September I went to France and took in a cargo of goods, but lost the lot.

On 12 November [1832], in company with my son, and two men, I went to sea and took up 25 kegs. At about 7 o'clock that evening we were chased and eventually captured by Lieutenant Buxton and his men. They came on board but found nothing. They hove the grappling irons overboard, but to no purpose. All they found was a piece of rope about one fathom in length, yet they took us into custody. They conveyed us to Lyme, and the next day we were taken before the mayor and the collector of customs. The preventive men were examined, and we were remanded until an order could be obtained from the board. It arrived on the 19th, and we were tried before the mayor and one of the magistrates for the county.

On this occasion, I employed two attorneys - Mr Flight and Mr Cann. The trial lasted from 2 o'clock till 8 o'clock. Nothing was sworn to but the piece of rope, yet we were found guilty and committed to Dorchester gaol, where we were conducted by Lieutenant Buxton and a riding officer.

The impression given by Rattenbury is that he was captured in 1831 when in fact it was in 1832. He was tried on 19 November 1832 at a cost to Customs of £24.12s. With him were his son William 30, Beer labourer William Abbot 31, and Beer fisherman Isaac Lane, 40. Being unable to pay the fines of £100 each, John Rattenbury, Abbot and

Lane were committed to prison and William Rattenbury was carried to a naval flag ship at Plymouth to be impressed. There he was judged unfit for naval service and within a week was on his way back to Dorchester.

The prison records describe John Rattenbury as having hair which was dark brown and grey, hazel eyes and a fair complexion. William Abbot was married with five children. His hair was light brown and he too had hazel eyes and a fair complexion. Isaac Lane, who was married with four children, had black hair, grey eyes and a swarthy complexion.

On 3 May 1833, William Rattenbury petitioned the Board for his release, but it was refused on the grounds that he was one of the most noted smugglers in the Lyme area. John Rattenbury petitioned the Board four months later in September 1833:

> *"Your Honorable petitioner, with the greatest contrition for his past faults, does acknowledge the crime for which he now suffers, and do most solemnly promise to your Lordships never more to be guilty of any offence against the Revenue Laws.*
>
> *Your humble petitioner sheweth that he is a man upwards of 58 years of age, and the father of ten children, two of which are afflicted and crippled. [They] have been supported by your humble petitioner without any assistance from the parish, which I am sorry to say, is now the case. Your humble petitioner has been confined upwards of eight months and do most humbly implore your Lordships' forgiveness, that I may again be able to return home to a disconsolate wife and an afflicted, helpless family."* (PRO. Lyme Letterbooks CUST 63/6)

There seem to be a couple of exaggerations in this petition. Rattenbury was not upwards of 58 years old but 55, and in September 1833 he had eight children not ten, most of them grown up. However, the youngest, Hannah may well have been afflicted for she was only six years old when she died in 1834. Elizabeth may not have been healthy either for she died in 1835, aged 13.

Asked to comment on Rattenbury's petition, the collector at Lyme described him as the 'oldest, most experienced, and incorrigible smuggler on this part of the coast, but from his infirmities (being subject to gout) he is not so active as formerly'. His petition did not succeed and he remained in gaol.

> In this situation I was employed as a watchman by night, and looked after the boys by day. The way I discharged these two duties gave great satisfaction to the governor, the chaplain, and the doctor, and the emolument arising from it tended very much to lessen the hardships I had to endure.

I remained in confinement until February 1833 [1834] when, through the kind offices of Mr Pinny, MP for Lyme, I once more tasted the sweets of liberty.

Colonel William Pinny of Somerton Erleigh in Somerset had been the MP for Lyme since 1831.

Isaac Lane and William Abbot were released in November 1833, but John Rattenbury had to wait until 1 February 1834. Two weeks later, a violent confrontation occurred on Beer beach between a large gang of smugglers and two preventive men.

By February 1834, Lt Buxton had been replaced as chief officer of the coastguard at Beer by Lt John Moor Bate RN. On 15 February, Bate's chief boatman, John Cornish, informed him that he had seen five men who left their cart on the road and then walked in the direction of Colyford. When he heard this, Bate suspected that a forced landing of smuggled goods was about to take place and sent word to the adjoining stations. Having been informed by Cornish that one of the men might have been armed, Bate supplied his men with six additional rounds of ball cartridge - making twenty each - before sending them out on night duty. He and Cornish patrolled the inland parts of the station together, going first to the westward. They returned to the watch house about midnight. At 1am, just as they were setting out again, an alarm was fired on Beer beach. They hurried there immediately. Meeting extraman Thomas Budden on the way, Bate directed him to follow.

When he arrived at the beach, Bate discovered an immense body of smugglers, about a hundred strong, some carrying tubs, others armed with large bludgeons, and determined to carry away their goods by force. Bate was equally determined to prevent them. Having discharged his pistol, he drew his cutlass, and seized a man who was carrying two tubs. The prisoner cried out to his colleagues for help, and a group of them, armed with sticks, came forward. They called out to Bate to release the prisoner, but he refused. He tried and failed to grab the nearest man. A smuggler swung a swingle at him, but Bate parried the blow with his cutlass. Surrounded now, Bate was seized and thrown down, and the cutlass wrested from his hand. The men kicked him repeatedly. 'Smother the bugger,' they said, banging his head on the shingle.

Thomas Budden, who was holding the smuggler previously seized, came to Bate's assistance. The prisoner took the opportunity to seize Bate's cutlass which Budden then tried to wrest from him. It was Bate's turn to go to Budden's assistance, and together they succeeded in securing the man.

The party of smugglers came on again so Bate threatened to shoot the first man to make a move towards him. That stopped them. They consulted amongst themselves, concluded they could not free their colleague, and left the beach. The boat of the *Swallow* cutter came ashore and the prisoner was taken aboard for safety, after which Bate collected the tubs on the beach. There were 61 half-ankers and three flagons. At daylight a couple more were found.

30. Beer beach

Were John and William Rattenbury involved in the smuggling incident which led to this confrontation? We don't know, but the majority of the men on the beach that night must have been from Beer and its locality.

In July 1834, William was acquitted of the charge of being concerned in unloading spirits from a boat on the grounds that there was insufficient evidence to convict him. James Orley and two Frenchmen - Pierre Chenatre, and Le Blond Bue - were discharged of being involved in the same landing, there being no more evidence available against them than there had been against William Rattenbury. It is not clear from Customs records when this smuggling incident occurred. Could it have been on Beer beach in the early hours of 16 February 1834?

In his memoirs, Rattenbury says nothing whatsoever about the confrontation even though it happened on his doorstep. His reticence is not surprising for he had reached a point in his narrative where he was relating events which occurred less than three years earlier. For the same reason he also neglected to tell his readers that one of his smuggling associates at the time was a member of the Mutter family of Beer.

William Rattenbury escaped a prison sentence in 1834, but the same cannot be said of Beer men Robert Gush 30, Henry Miller 28, Jacob Gibbs 39, and Henry Gibbs, convicted of a separate smuggling offence on 8 August and sent to Dorchester Prison. There they joined two other locals - Thomas Miller 34 and John Tidbury 18.

A month after the affray on Beer beach, John Rattenbury was off to Cherbourg again.

> In the following March [1834], I again embarked on a voyage to Cherbourg, returning with a cargo of spirits. Half was sunk and lost; the remainder was landed and concealed among the cliffs for three days and nights, and at last conveyed away by daylight.
>
> I made my next, and last, voyage to Cherbourg in October the same year [1834]. On my return I sent a man on shore to procure assistance, but he was unfortunately taken by some of the preventive men. I therefore sunk the kegs myself, but lost the whole because I was laid up with a fit of the gout.

According to Lt W Marshall of the *Nimble* revenue cutter, Rattenbury went over to France for a cargo of contraband two months later at the end of December 1834. The boat he used was the *Hannah*, owned by Beer fisherman William Mutter, which was seized by Marshall on 26 December 1834 for not being properly licensed.

On 6 January 1835, Mutter petitioned for the boat's return. He was supported by local merchants Frederick Holmes and William Head, two churchwardens, and by William Pole who wrote from Shute House assuring Customs that every syllable in Mutter's petition was true.

Lt Marshall and W Usherwood, the inspecting commander of the coastguard who was based at Lyme, were less inclined to trust in Mutter's veracity. Marshall explained to the Board that on 25 December 1834 he had communicated with Usherwood, and with the chief officer of the Beer station, who informed him that the boat *Hannah* had gone across to what he described as the 'otherside' for a cargo of contraband spirits on the Tuesday night. With her was 'the notorious Rattenbury'. Usherword confirmed this:

> *"On 24th of the said month, I received information I could rely on that the* Hannah *had sailed from Beer at 1am on that morning on a smuggling trip, with Rattenbury, a notorious smuggler, and three other men in her, and that they were determined to force a landing. My having given the necessary directions to the Officers under my orders, we anxiously waited her arrival, and at 1am on 26 December, a strong party of smugglers was discovered near*

Branscombe. Also a fire signal had been made by them at Beer Head. The Nimble, *which was cruising near that spot, stood out to sea and at 9am, from the mast head saw a boat, which she chased. She proved to be the* Hannah *with Rattenbury and three others on board [including William Mutter].*

Agreeable to our information at this time, it appears she smelled strong of spirits. Finding that she had no licence on board, Lt Marshall, the commander of the Nimble, *seized her.*

There is not the slightest doubt in my mind that this boat Hannah *had been across for smuggled goods, and that she was made to throw them out on the morning of 26 December when chased by the* Nimble. *From the newness of the tubs picked up two days afterwards by the crew of the Teignmouth station, it is clear they had been but a short time in the water, and I have every reason to believe that they were a part of the* Hannah's *cargo."*
(PRO. Exeter Letterbooks CUST 64/40)

By 1835, the positions of John and William Rattenbury appear to have been reversed with John helping in William's ventures instead of the other way round.

In June 1835, under the pretence of catching mackerel, I went out in a boat at about 11 o'clock in the morning to pick up some kegs which my son had sunk. I landed them in two halves at Charton Bay [between Lyme and Seaton] where people were there to receive them. Just as we were returning, we met two boats belonging to the coastguard. They were going out to secure the tubs, since which time two men have been stationed at the place we landed.

J M Bate's report of 24 June 1835 to the collector at Lyme shows that he was looking for tubs in the same area, and at roughly the same time as Rattenbury. On 17 June 1835, while at the Beer station, he received a note from Thomas Stocker, chief officer of the Axmouth coastguard station, passing on information received about a raft of tubs which had been sunk by smugglers at either Culverhole or Charton Bay. It was believed that the smugglers intended to retrieve and land them that very night using a stone boat called the *Fish*, belonging to Thomas Colman of Seaton, 'an old and notorious smuggler'.

That night Bate and his men, while patrolling the area in their boat, encountered the *Fish*, manned by John Burford (known as 'Uncle Jack'), John Start and Phillip Garrett, all of Axmouth, and Thomas Carter of Weymouth (who gave a false name). Bate examined their boat. He found in it a creeper and fifty fathoms of wet rope, and noted that the vessel's paintwork had been rendered and altered in such a way as to make her less visible; but none of this warranted him holding the boat or her crew. However, he did not give up on the tubs, and with the help of the Branscombe station boat searched for them. At 4pm they were found just forty yards from the buoy which Bate had dropped to mark the spot where the *Fish* had been boarded.

It is quite possible that, after returning from his own successful landing in Charton Bay, Rattenbury saw the Beer and Branscombe preventive boats on the way out to spoil the landing of Colman's goods, which had been sunk in the same area.

> In the beginning of January 1836, I went to Torquay in a cart to collect twenty tubs of brandy which we then took to Newton Bushel [now part of Newton Abbot. It was amalgamated in 1902 after changing its name to Highweek]. Someone found out about it and informed on us, therefore, at 10 o'clock at night, about a mile out of Newton Bushel, officers on horseback came up. One of the them took hold of the horse's reins. "I seize this horse and cart on behalf of the king and myself," he said. As soon as I heard this, I made my escape, but the man who owned the cart was arrested and taken to Exeter.
>
> That was how my career as a smuggler ended.

The owner of the horse and cart was Samuel Pike who was sent to gaol at Exeter from where, on 5 March 1836, he offered the Exeter collector information about those who had been involved with him. He claimed that George Gibbs and John Rattenbury, both fishermen of Beer, and John Bolt, a sawyer of Tor near Torquay, had been with him when he was arrested but had made their escape. He also said that Robert Cornish, a coal dealer of Tor, was also concerned and that it was from his house that he had taken up ten of the casks of spirits which were found his cart. John Bolt had assisted in removing another ten casks from his own property - a garden between Tor and Torquay - and these were also in Pike's cart.

Pike's deposition, which was sent to the Board, was accompanied by a letter from Exeter Customs stating that Gibbs and Rattenbury were 'very suspicious characters', but on 10 March Pike had to admit he had no evidence to corroborate his claim. The matter was taken no further and Rattenbury narrowly escaped another prison sentence.

CHAPTER 20

Smuggling Methods;
another Court Appearance
1836-1844

Rattenbury is coming to the end of his narrative but only now does he reveal some of the devices he used in smuggling. He may have been prompted by his publisher who must by now have realised how uninformative Rattenbury's *Memoirs* were going to be in this respect.

However much smuggling may gratify a hardy and enterprising spirit and call forth all the latent energies of the soul, it is also fraught with difficulty and danger. Many and various have been the expedients I have used to escape detection, baffle pursuit, and eluded the vigilance of those indefatigable picaroons which everywhere line our coasts.

On one occasion I had a goose on board, which the master who overhauled the vessel was very desirous of buying, but I was too well aware of the value of the stuffing to part with it, for instead of onions and sage, it consisted of fine lace.

About the same time I had stowed some valuable French silks in a tin box, which was soldered to prevent the water from getting in. While an officer was searching another part of the vessel, I contrived to throw it overboard, having previously attached to it a stone and a buoy, by which means I recovered the silks perfect and uninjured.

Having landed a cargo at Seaton Hole one dark night, I was going up the cliff with a keg at my back when I had the ill-luck to stumble over an ass. It began to bray so horribly that, together with the noise occasioned by my fall, an officer who was taking a nap below awoke, in consequence of which he seized nearly forty kegs, being the whole of the cargo.

One day, hearing that my son, who I had sent to Seaton with a flagon of brandy, had been taken by a preventive man, I seized a poker and ran out to effect his rescue, but found he had escaped observation through climbing up into a tree.

To these examples I might add many more of a similar nature.

I have also experienced the greatest vicissitudes. My spirits have been alternatively elated by success, and depressed by misfortune, but through it all I never yielded to despair, for hope always cheered me and illuminated my way even at the darkest times.

The last time I appeared in a public court was at Exeter assizes, held in March 1836, as a witness on behalf of my son [William] who was charged, with others, of having been engaged in an affray on

Budleigh Salterton beach on 1 December 1835 when William Noble Clay and John Bachelor, officers in His Majesty's customs, were assaulted, maltreated, and obstructed in the discharge of their duty.

Lt Clay was the chief officer of the coastguard at Budleigh Salterton, and John Bachelor was his chief boatman. They were assaulted on the morning of Wednesday 2 December 1835, but managed to seize 52 tubs of brandy and geneva. William Rattenbury, who was identified by Lt Clay as one of the men who tied and bound him, was arrested on the morning of Saturday 5 December as he was crossing the Exe ferry. Arrested at Awliscombe near Honiton, and charged with the same offence, was Henry Bird. Both men were remanded in custody and sent to Exeter gaol to await trial at the next assizes. The collector at Exeter referred to the incident in a report to the Board about the state of smuggling in his district:

> "One run only has been attempted on this coast in the last quarter. [It] was accompanied with acts of violence towards the coastguard officers stationed at Budleigh Salterton, who succeeded in capturing the boat of goods after a fight with the smugglers, some of whom are now under prosecution.
> A small quantity of smuggled spirits, which it is supposed had been sunk to the eastward of this port, broke adrift in a gale of wind [and] drifted ashore upon Dawlish beach. Some trifling seizures have also been made by the officers of Excise inland, but these we have no reason to believe were landed within the limits of this port, nor do we think any other circumstance of smuggling has occurred within this port during the quarter ended 5 January 1836. (PRO. Exeter Letterbooks CUST 64/40, 13 January 1836)

If the collector's intelligence was accurate then smuggling was in decline, of which the violent incidents on Beer and Budleigh Salterton beaches were symptoms. The smugglers, faced with a much enlarged and more effective coastguard, had, perhaps out of desperation, banded together to try to protect the landing of their cargos. But not even these tactics achieved their end - as happened at Budleigh Salterton, the coastguard seized the goods anyway.

It is significant that a Beer man (William Rattenbury) features so strongly in the one major smuggling incident in three months recorded on the coast between Teignmouth and Axmouth, because when it came to smuggling, Beer was always first in, last out.

The case [against William in March 1836] excited considerable interest. Numerous witnesses were examined and they all testified that he was at Beer sixteen miles away at the time of the incident, but to no avail. He was found guilty and sentenced to seven years' transportation.

170

Some gentlemen of consequence narrowly investigated the case and, convinced of his innocence, signed several petitions, which were sent to Lord John Russell. He presented them to the King, who graciously granted him a royal pardon.

On the occasion of his trial, I was examined by Mr Sergeant Bompas. It caused a great deal of amusement at the time, so I have extracted the following passages from a newspaper which contained an account of the trial.

"I keep school at sea - fish for sole, turbot and brill; any kind of fish that comes to hook."

"Which do you catch oftenest, sole or tub?"

"Oh, the devil, a tub (great laughter); there are too many picaroons going now-a-day."

"You have caught a good many in your time?"

"Ah plenty of it! I wish you and I had as much of it as we could drink."

"You have kept school at home, and trained up your son?"

"I have always trained him up in a regular honourable way, larnt him the creed, the Lord's prayer, and the ten commandments."

"You don't find there, Thou shalt not smuggle?"

"No, but I find there, Thou shalt not bear false witness against thy neighbour."

"Nobody smuggles now-a-day?"

"Don't they though!" (laughter)

"So these horses at Beer cannot go above three or four miles an hour?"

"If you had not better horses, you would never get to London. I seldom ride a horse-back. If I do, I generally fall off seven or eight times in a journey." (Great laughter).

Since I left off smuggling I have been principally engaged in fishing and piloting. Lately, however, I have entered into an engagement for conveying the blue lias lime, and the stone, for the harbour which is in contemplation at Sidmouth.

The Bill to build a harbour at Sidmouth was read in the House of Commons for the first time in 1825 and received the Royal Assent in July 1836, but, like the proposed harbour at Beer, it was never built.

As a pilot I have, under Divine Providence, been instrumental in saving many vessels from being wrecked. One such instant occurred only a short time ago. However, it is likely to cause me some inconvenience because, after I had saved the vessel, a person who went on board told the captain that I, and those who had assisted me, were the very men who would rob him. My passions were so roused that I struck him, and have since been served a summons to appear before the magistrates. As I took no notice of that, I have since received another.

And this, apart from the following homage to Lord Rolle -

The Smuggler gratefully acknowledges the kindness of the Right Hon Lord Rolle, who has allowed him one shilling per week for life -

is where Rattenbury ends his story.

Lord Rolle also allowed Rattenbury the tenancy of one of his Beer cottages. It was situated close to the beach, a few houses along what is now called Common Lane.

In 1841 when the first national census was taken, William Rattenbury and his wife Susannah were living in Main Street, as was Abraham Mutter 65 (described as an agricultural labourer), and his grand-daughter Ann 20. The names of Orley, Phillips, Loveridge, Abbot, Farrant, Russell, Miller, Driver, Puttam and Lane are also well represented.

John Rattenbury's mother, the former Anne Newton, lived to be 87. She died in 1839 only five years before her son. Daniel French died in 1835 aged 76, Abraham Mutter in 1842, and William Loveridge in 1842, aged 72. John Rattenbury died two years later in 1844, and was buried on 28 April. He was 65.

31. Fore St, Beer today

EPILOGUE

John Rattenbury may well have given up smuggling in 1836, but other men in the Beer area carried on as before, despite being under close surveillance by the coastguard. The trade did not fall into a terminal decline until the 1840s when the government reduced the duty on a wide range of items. Thereafter it was so much less profitable that the field was left to only to the most incorrigible smugglers which, of course, the Beer men were!

At 1am on 30 November 1843 two revenue cutters, the *Adelaide* and the *Asp*, encountered a suspicious French vessel called *Le Pierre* of Cherbourg, which they suspected of having sent a boat containing a cargo of spirits ashore under Beer Head. A tub boat was later found with five half-ankers on board. Lt Drew of the coastguard at Branscombe also found 101 ankers sunk half a mile out to sea. Both seizures were believed to have come from the *Pierre*. If oral testimony is to be believed, then the smugglers involved were probably those led by Rattenbury's successor, Samuel Mutter.

In 1956, J R W Coxhead gathered together in a small book called *Smuggling Days in Devon*, the oral accounts of several east Devon smugglers and their descendants. Their testimony consistently points to the involvement of the Mutter family not only in smuggling, but in association with John Rattenbury.

As a Beer family, the Mutters did not have the pedigree of the Newtons and Gibbs. The first to be recorded in the parish was Samuel Mutter (probably born in neighbouring Northleigh in 1744) who in 1768 married a Beer woman called Rebecca Gregory. They had at least five children - Elizabeth (1768) who married Joshua Miller, William (1770) who married Joanna Westlake, George (1772), Samuel (1774) and Abraham (1777). The three youngest also married and had families.

Some of these Mutter brothers were certainly smugglers. In 1816 William and George were both described as such by William Gibbs, and it was William Mutter who owned and was sailing with Rattenbury in the *Hannah* when it was seized by the *Nimble* revenue cutter in December 1834. But what about Samuel Jnr?

It is Samuel who is believed to have taken over from Rattenbury when he retired. Coxhead describes him as a bold and experienced sailor who landed cargos at night at isolated spots on the coast between Exmouth and Seaton. And Samuel's brother Abraham is reputed to have been responsible for conveying the contraband inland, and for selling it to their many customers in east Devon.

In my research in the Customs letterbooks for Devon and Dorset I have not once come across the name of Abraham Mutter of Beer in connection with smuggling. Other sources, however, cite him as being heavily involved. On 11 May 1956, the *Western Times & Gazette* carried an article which described him as a turf-cutter and wood merchant who carried on his trade on land near Peak Hill in Sidmouth, the land known today as Mutter's Moor. With several carts and a team of donkeys he is supposed to have hawked his wares over a wide area, selling them in Sidmouth, Exmouth, even as far as Exeter. The article credits Rattenbury with the idea of hiding and conveying contraband under Abraham's turfs, and from then on, and for many years afterwards, Mutter is believed to have co-operated fully in Rattenbury's smuggling enterprises. His son John joined the 'family business', and it is he who has the dubious of honour of being the last man in the West Country to earn his living from smuggling.

Another piece of land in the Sidmouth area is also associated with the name Mutter. It was known in 1809 as Churchyard Field. On 15 March 1809, an Abraham Mutter took a 61-year lease on it from Samuel Cowley, but there is no evidence to suggest that the leaseholder was Abraham Mutter of Beer.

Coxhead derived some of his information from J Y Anderson-Morshead's *History of Salcombe Regis* which included the testimonies of Salcombe parishioners, some of whom had been involved in, or knew of smuggling in their area in the first half of the 19th Century. One of these witnesses was Robert Channon, a sexton of Salcombe Regis. Born in 1803, he stated that the main smuggler in the area was 'Mutter of Harcombe who kept a public [house] in Exmouth' and who was 'more artful than Rattenbury'. He remembered that two Branscombe farmers - Bray and Williams - also smuggled.

Henry Northcote, another witness, who was born in 1819, remembered the two Branscombe farmers as Bray and Fry, and said they were the mainstays of the business. Northcote himself admitted to having carried up the cliffs scores of tubs which were then shouldered into a pit at Paccombe bottom where a lid was put over them. One consignment was hidden in a cellar at Slade, a farm in the area.

Northcote said that Rattenbury brought goods over from France in a cutter called *Primrose* which had once been a gentleman's yacht, and though she was taken often by the coastguard, her papers were always right and she was released, but she was eventually caught and sawed in half because that was the only way the customs men could stop her smuggling. 'I knew Rattenbury and have heard that he cut the officer up for crab bait, but he always laughed if it was thrown up at him', said Northcote. Although he may have known Rattenbury personally in his later years, Northcote was too young to have had first-hand knowledge of anything but a few of his later smuggling ventures. Farmer Samuel Bray of Woodhead, however, was smuggling in 1857, fourteen years after Rattenbury's death therefore Northcote's testimony about him is not only more immediate and reliable, but is supported by the testimony of others, including Robert Channon.

Daniel Hooper, born in 1831 in the valley of the Offwell brook, was also involved with the Branscombe smugglers of the 1850s, and used to help to bring brandy kegs ashore and carry them inland. He described how the goods were landed at the base of a sheer cliff and hauled up precariously on a platform formed from a farm gate with ropes tied to each corner.

Paccombe Bottom was the site of one storage pit but, according to Coxhead, there were others. In a field at Branscombe, the smugglers are reputed to have dug diagonal shafts into the ground to a depth of about 12ft and at the bottom hollowed out a chamber about 10ft in diameter to store their contraband. In September 1953, Mr Clement Ford, Lord of the Manor of Branscombe, showed Coxhead an estate map on which was marked the positions of about six of these underground chambers. They had been discovered between 1909 and 1939 during farming operations.

Bovey House was believed to have been used to store contraband in an earlier period - at the end of the 18th Century when the building was empty. In her book *Smuggling in Devon and Cornwall 1700-1850*, Mary Waugh says that there was one storage chamber beside the chimney and another 30ft down a well.

Bovey House still stands. It is a hotel for visitors. And caravans now sit atop Beer Head where so many fires were once lit by smugglers' accomplices to warn their comrades at sea. The population of Beer is much larger now but the layout of the principal streets has changed little since Rattenbury's time. And off season, the town retains the quiet and sleepy air described by the Reverend John Swete in 1794.

Sitting in Jubilee Gardens - where surely in the early 1800s, riding officer Robert Head's house was situated - it isn't difficult to imagine an Alderney smuggling cutter anchored in the bay, and tub boats launching from the beach below to go off to her to bring her contraband ashore, nor to gauge the eagerness with which local people would clean up their beach after a storm had uprooted from the seabed and thrown onto it items rather more desirable than rusting beer cans!

It is more difficult for us to imagine the strains which in the early 19th century the mariners of Beer and their families experienced in the face of recessionary influences, when their employment opportunities were few except in ventures that were both illegal and hazardous. Their choices were limited. We live in more affluent times, but we should always be alert to the lessons of human experience that history proffers us, because if such socially difficult times are allowed to come again, the lives of ordinary people will once more be blighted by a criminality which is born out of need, not greed.

32. John Rattenbury (from his Memoirs *1837)*

BIBLIOGRAPHY

COXE, A D HIPPISLEY — A Book about Smuggling in the West Country 1700-1850. Tabb House, 1984.

COXHEAD, J R W — Smuggling Days in Devon. Raleigh Press, Exmouth, 1956.

CROWHURST, F — The French War on Trade: privateering 1793-1815. Scholar Press, 1989.

DICKINSON, M G Ed. — A Living from the Sea: Devon's Fishing Industry and its Fishermen. Devon Books 1987.

EADIE, P M — The Channel Islands. Rand McNally, 1981.

FORSYTHE, W J — A System of Discipline - Exeter Borough Prison 1819-1863. University of Exeter, 1983.

GUTTRIDGE, R — Dorset Smugglers. Dorset Publishing, 1987.

HARDY, C — The Smuggler's Guide to Purbeck

HUNT, P E — Devon's Age of Elegance. Devon Books, 1984.

MARCUS, G J — Heart of Oak: a survey of British sea power in the Georgian era. OUP, 1965.

MARR, L J — A History of the Bailiwick of Guernsey. Phillimore, 1982

MORLEY, G — Smuggling in Hampshire & Dorset 1700-1850. Countryside Books. Revised edition 1990.

RATTENBURY, J — Memoirs of a Smuggler. J Harvey, Sidmouth 1837

SHORE, H N — Smuggling Days and Smuggling Ways. Cassell 1892

SMITH, G — King's Cutters: the Revenue Service and the War against Smuggling. Conway/Maritime Press, 1983.

WAUGH, M — Smuggling in Devon and Cornwall 1700-1850. Countryside Books, 1991.

Castle St Exeter EX4 3PQ

Will send photocopy with invoice

WEST COUNTRY STUDIES LIBRARY, Devon 01392 384216
  Exeter Flying Post
  Devon Notes and Queries Vol.IV, pp 257-260. French Prisoners in Tiverton
  1797-1811, by Emily Skinner

DEVON RECORD OFFICE. Exeter 01392 384253
  Shipping Registers - Dartmouth, Exeter
  Beer and Seaton Tithe Map 1840, Census 1841, Parish Registers, etc

COUNTY RECORD OFFICE, Dorchester
  Shipping Registers - Lyme, Weymouth
  Parish Registers - Lyme, Burton Bradstock, etc
  Pigot's Directories

PUBLIC RECORD OFFICE, Kew
  Customs Letterbooks: Cowes, Poole, Weymouth, Lyme, Exeter, Dartmouth

INDEX